ASPEN PUBLISHERS

Casenote™ Legal Briefs

PROFESSIONAL RESPONSIBILITY

Keyed to Courses Using

Hazard, Koniak, Cramton, Cohen, and Wendel's
The Law and Ethics of Lawyering

Fifth Edition

Wolters Kluwer
Law & Business

AUSTIN BOSTON CHICAGO NEW YORK THE NETHERLANDS

This publication is designed to provide accurate and authoritative information in regard to the subject matter covered. It is sold with the understanding that the publisher is not engaged in rendering legal, accounting, or other professional services. If legal advice or other expert assistance is required, the services of a competent professional person should be sought.

— From a Declaration of Principles adopted jointly by a Committee of the American Bar Association and a Committee of Publishers and Associates

www.AspenLaw.com

To contact Customer Care, e-mail customer.service@aspenpublishers.com, call 1-800-234-1660, fax 1-800-901-9075, or mail correspondence to:

Aspen Publishers
Attn: Order Department
P.O. Box 990
Frederick, MD 21705

Printed in the United States of America.

1 2 3 4 5 6 7 8 9 0

ISBN 978-0-7355-9910-9

About Wolters Kluwer Law & Business

Wolters Kluwer Law & Business is a leading provider of research information and workflow solutions in key specialty areas. The strengths of the individual brands of Aspen Publishers, CCH, Kluwer Law International and Loislaw are aligned within Wolters Kluwer Law & Business to provide comprehensive, in-depth solutions and expert-authored content for the legal, professional and education markets.

CCH was founded in 1913 and has served more than four generations of business professionals and their clients. The CCH products in the Wolters Kluwer Law & Business group are highly regarded electronic and print resources for legal, securities, antitrust and trade regulation, government contracting, banking, pension, payroll, employment and labor, and health-care reimbursement and compliance professionals.

Aspen Publishers is a leading information provider for attorneys, business professionals and law students. Written by preeminent authorities, Aspen products offer analytical and practical information in a range of specialty practice areas from securities law and intellectual property to mergers and acquisitions and pension/benefits. Aspen's trusted legal education resources provide professors and students with high-quality, up-to-date and effective resources for successful instruction and study in all areas of the law.

Kluwer Law International supplies the global business community with comprehensive English-language international legal information. Legal practitioners, corporate counsel and business executives around the world rely on the Kluwer Law International journals, loose-leafs, books and electronic products for authoritative information in many areas of international legal practice.

Loislaw is a premier provider of digitized legal content to small law firm practitioners of various specializations. Loislaw provides attorneys with the ability to quickly and efficiently find the necessary legal information they need, when and where they need it, by facilitating access to primary law as well as state-specific law, records, forms and treatises.

Wolters Kluwer Law & Business, a unit of Wolters Kluwer, is headquartered in New York and Riverwoods, Illinois. Wolters Kluwer is a leading multinational publisher and information services company.

Format for the Casenote Legal Brief

Nature of Case: This section identifies the form of action (e.g., breach of contract, negligence, battery), the type of proceeding (e.g., demurrer, appeal from trial court's jury instructions), or the relief sought (e.g., damages, injunction, criminal sanctions).

Fact Summary: This is included to refresh your memory and can be used as a quick reminder of the facts.

Rule of Law: Summarizes the general principle of law that the case illustrates. It may be used for instant recall of the court's holding and for classroom discussion or home review.

Facts: This section contains all relevant facts of the case, including the contentions of the parties and the lower court holdings. It is written in a logical order to give the student a clear understanding of the case. The plaintiff and defendant are identified by their proper names throughout and are always labeled with a (P) or (D).

Party ID: Quick identification of the relationship between the parties.

Concurrence/Dissent: All concurrences and dissents are briefed whenever they are included by the casebook editor.

Analysis: This last paragraph gives you a broad understanding of where the case "fits in" with other cases in the section of the book and with the entire course. It is a hornbook-style discussion indicating whether the case is a majority or minority opinion and comparing the principal case with other cases in the casebook. It may also provide analysis from restatements, uniform codes, and law review articles. The analysis will prove to be invaluable to classroom discussion.

Palsgraf v. Long Island R.R. Co.

Injured bystander (P) v. Railroad company (D)

N.Y. Ct. App., 248 N.Y. 339, 162 N.E. 99 (1928).

NATURE OF CASE: Appeal from judgment affirming verdict for plaintiff seeking damages for personal injury.

FACT SUMMARY: Helen Palsgraf (P) was injured on R.R.'s (D) train platform when R.R.'s (D) guard helped a passenger aboard a moving train, causing his package to fall on the tracks. The package contained fireworks which exploded, creating a shock that tipped a scale onto Palsgraf (P).

RULE OF LAW

The risk reasonably to be perceived defines the duty to be obeyed.

FACTS: Helen Palsgraf (P) purchased a ticket to Rockaway Beach from R.R. (D) and was waiting on the train platform. As she waited, two men ran to catch a train that was pulling out from the platform. The first man jumped aboard, but the second man, who appeared as if he might fall, was helped aboard by the guard on the train who had kept the door open so they could jump aboard. A guard on the platform also helped by pushing him onto the train. The man was carrying a package wrapped in newspaper. In the process, the man dropped his package, which fell on the tracks. The package contained fireworks and exploded. The shock of the explosion was apparently of great enough strength to tip over some scales at the other end of the platform, which fell on Palsgraf (P) and injured her. A jury awarded her damages, and R.R. (D) appealed.

ISSUE: Does the risk reasonably to be perceived define the duty to be obeyed?

HOLDING AND DECISION: (Cardozo, C.J.) Yes. The risk reasonably to be perceived defines the duty to be obeyed. If there is no foreseeable hazard to the injured party as the result of a seemingly innocent act, the act does not become a tort because it happened to be a wrong as to another. If the wrong was not willful, the plaintiff must show that the act as to her had such great and apparent possibilities of danger as to entitle her to protection. Negligence in the abstract is not enough upon which to base liability. Negligence is a relative concept, evolving out of the common law doctrine of trespass on the case. To establish liability, the defendant must owe a legal duty of reasonable care to the injured party. A cause of action in tort will lie where harm, though unintended, could have been averted or avoided by observance of such a duty. The scope of the duty is limited by the range of danger that a reasonable person could foresee. In this case, there was nothing to suggest from the appearance of the parcel or otherwise that the parcel contained fireworks. The guard could not reasonably have had any warning of a threat to Palsgraf (P), and R.R. (D) therefore cannot be held liable. Judgment is reversed in favor of R.R. (D).

DISSENT: (Andrews, J.) The concept that there is no negligence unless R.R. (D) owes a legal duty to take care as to Palsgraf (P) herself is too narrow. Everyone owes to the world at large the duty of refraining from those acts that may unreasonably threaten the safety of others. If the guard's action was negligent as to those nearby, it was also negligent as to those outside what might be termed the "danger zone." For Palsgraf (P) to recover, R.R.'s (D) negligence must have been the proximate cause of her injury, a question of fact for the jury.

ANALYSIS

The majority defined the limit of the defendant's liability in terms of the danger that a reasonable person in defendant's situation would have perceived. The dissent argued that the limitation should not be placed on liability, but rather on damages. Judge Andrews suggested that only injuries that would not have happened but for R.R.'s (D) negligence should be compensable. Both the majority and dissent recognized the policy-driven need to limit liability for negligent acts, seeking, in the words of Judge Andrews, to define a framework "that will be practical and in keeping with the general understanding of mankind." The Restatement (Second) of Torts has accepted Judge Cardozo's view.

Quicknotes

FORESEEABILITY A reasonable expectation that change is the probable result of certain acts or omissions

NEGLIGENCE Conduct falling below the standard of care that a reasonable person would demonstrate under similar conditions.

PROXIMATE CAUSE The natural sequence of events without which an injury would not have been sustained.

Issue: The issue is a concise question that brings out the essence of the opinion as it relates to the section of the casebook in which the case appears. Both substantive and procedural issues are included if relevant to the decision.

Holding and Decision: This section offers a clear and in-depth discussion of the rule of the case and the court's rationale. It is written in easy-to-understand language and answers the issue presented by applying the law to the facts of the case. When relevant, it includes a thorough discussion of the exceptions to the case as listed by the court, any major cites to the other cases on point, and the names of the judges who wrote the decisions.

Quicknotes: Conveniently defines legal terms found in the case and summarizes the nature of any statutes, codes, or rules referred to in the text.

Note to Students

Aspen Publishers is proud to offer *Casenote Legal Briefs*—continuing thirty years of publishing America's best-selling legal briefs.

Casenote Legal Briefs are designed to help you save time when briefing assigned cases. Organized under convenient headings, they show you how to abstract the basic facts and holdings from the text of the actual opinions handed down by the courts. Used as part of a rigorous study regimen, they can help you spend more time analyzing and critiquing points of law than on copying bits and pieces of judicial opinions into your notebook or outline.

Casenote Legal Briefs should never be used as a substitute for assigned casebook readings. They work best when read as a follow-up to reviewing the underlying opinions themselves. Students who try to avoid reading and digesting the judicial opinions in their casebooks or online sources will end up shortchanging themselves in the long run. The ability to absorb, critique, and restate the dynamic and complex elements of case law decisions is crucial to your success in law school and beyond. It cannot be developed vicariously.

Casenote Legal Briefs represents but one of the many offerings in Aspen's Study Aid Timeline, which includes:

- *Casenote Legal Briefs*
- *Emanuel Law Outlines*
- *Examples & Explanations* Series
- *Introduction to Law* Series
- Emanuel *Law in a Flash* Flash Cards
- Emanuel *CrunchTime* Series

Each of these series is designed to provide you with easy-to-understand explanations of complex points of law. Each volume offers guidance on the principles of legal analysis and, consulted regularly, will hone your ability to spot relevant issues. We have titles that will help you prepare for class, prepare for your exams, and enhance your general comprehension of the law along the way.

To find out more about Aspen Study Aid publications, visit us online at *www.AspenLaw.com* or email us at *legaledu@wolterskluwer.com.* We'll be happy to assist you.

Get this Casenote Legal Brief as an AspenLaw Studydesk eBook today!

By returning this form to Aspen Publishers, you will receive a complimentary eBook download of this Casenote Legal Brief and AspenLaw Studydesk productivity software.* Learn more about AspenLaw Studydesk today at *www.AspenLaw.com/Studydesk.*

Name		**Phone** ( )	
Address			**Apt. No.**
City		**State**	**ZIP Code**
Law School		**Graduation Date** Month ______ Year ______	

Cut out the UPC found on the lower left corner of the back cover of this book. Staple the UPC inside this box. Only the original UPC from the book cover will be accepted. (No photocopies or store stickers are allowed.)

Attach UPC inside this box.

Email (Print legibly or you may not get access!)
Title of this book (course subject)
ISBN of this book (10- or 13-digit number on the UPC)
Used with which casebook (provide author's name)

Mail the completed form to:

Aspen Publishers, Inc.
Legal Education Division
130 Turner Street, Bldg 3, 4th Floor
Waltham, MA 02453-8901

* Upon receipt of this completed form, you will be emailed a code for the digital download of this book in AspenLaw Studydesk eBook format and a free copy of the software application, which is required to read the eBook.

For a full list of eBook study aids available for AspenLaw Studydesk software and other resources that will help you with your law school studies, visit *www.AspenLaw.com.*

Make a photocopy of this form and your UPC for your records.

For detailed information on the use of the information you provide on this form, please see the PRIVACY POLICY at *www.AspenLaw.com.*

How to Brief a Case

A. Decide on a Format and Stick to It

Structure is essential to a good brief. It enables you to arrange systematically the related parts that are scattered throughout most cases, thus making manageable and understandable what might otherwise seem to be an endless and unfathomable sea of information. There are, of course, an unlimited number of formats that can be utilized. However, it is best to find one that suits your needs and stick to it. Consistency breeds both efficiency and the security that when called upon you will know where to look in your brief for the information you are asked to give.

Any format, as long as it presents the essential elements of a case in an organized fashion, can be used. Experience, however, has led *Casenotes* to develop and utilize the following format because of its logical flow and universal applicability.

NATURE OF CASE: This is a brief statement of the legal character and procedural status of the case (e.g., "Appeal of a burglary conviction").

There are many different alternatives open to a litigant dissatisfied with a court ruling. The key to determining which one has been used is to discover *who is asking this court for what.*

This first entry in the brief should be kept as *short as possible.* Use the court's terminology if you understand it. But since jurisdictions vary as to the titles of pleadings, the best entry is the one that addresses who wants what in this proceeding, not the one that sounds most like the court's language.

RULE OF LAW: A statement of the general principle of law that the case illustrates (e.g., "An acceptance that varies any term of the offer is considered a rejection and counteroffer").

Determining the rule of law of a case is a procedure similar to determining the issue of the case. Avoid being fooled by red herrings; there may be a few rules of law mentioned in the case excerpt, but usually only one is *the* rule with which the casebook editor is concerned. The techniques used to locate the issue, described below, may also be utilized to find the rule of law. Generally, your best guide is simply the chapter heading. It is a clue to the point the casebook editor seeks to make and should be kept in mind when reading every case in the respective section.

FACTS: A synopsis of only the essential facts of the case, i.e., those bearing upon or leading up to the issue.

The facts entry should be a short statement of the events and transactions that led one party to initiate legal proceedings against another in the first place. While some cases conveniently state the salient facts at the beginning of the decision, in other instances they will have to be culled from hiding places throughout the text, even from concurring and dissenting opinions. Some of the "facts" will often be in dispute and should be so noted. Conflicting evidence may be briefly pointed up. "Hard" facts must be included. Both must be *relevant* in order to be listed in the facts entry. It is impossible to tell what is relevant until the entire case is read, as the ultimate determination of the rights and liabilities of the parties may turn on something buried deep in the opinion.

Generally, the facts entry should not be longer than three to five *short* sentences.

It is often helpful to identify the role played by a party in a given context. For example, in a construction contract case the identification of a party as the "contractor" or "builder" alleviates the need to tell that that party was the one who was supposed to have built the house.

It is always helpful, and a good general practice, to identify the "plaintiff" and the "defendant." This may seem elementary and uncomplicated, but, especially in view of the creative editing practiced by some casebook editors, it is sometimes a difficult or even impossible task. Bear in mind that the *party presently* seeking something from this court may not be the plaintiff, and that sometimes only the cross-claim of a defendant is treated in the excerpt. Confusing or misaligning the parties can ruin your analysis and understanding of the case.

ISSUE: A statement of the general legal question answered by or illustrated in the case. For clarity, the issue is best put in the form of a question capable of a "yes" or "no" answer. In reality, the issue is simply the Rule of Law put in the form of a question (e.g., "May an offer be accepted by performance?").

The major problem presented in discerning what is *the* issue in the case is that an opinion usually purports to raise and answer several questions. However, except for rare cases, only one such question is really the issue in the case. Collateral issues not necessary to the resolution of the matter in controversy are handled by the court by language known as *"obiter dictum"* or merely *"dictum."* While dicta may be included later in the brief, they have no place under the issue heading.

To find the issue, ask *who wants what* and then go on to ask *why did that party succeed or fail in getting it.* Once this is determined, the "why" should be turned into a question.

The complexity of the issues in the cases will vary, but in all cases a single-sentence question should sum up the issue. *In a few cases,* there will be two, or even more rarely, three issues of equal importance to the resolution of the case. Each should be expressed in a single-sentence question.

Since many issues are resolved by a court in coming to a final disposition of a case, the casebook editor will reproduce the portion of the opinion containing the issue or issues most relevant to the area of law under scrutiny. A noted law professor gave this advice: "Close the book; look at the title on the cover." Chances are, if it is Property, you need not concern yourself with whether, for example, the federal government's treatment of the plaintiff's land really raises a federal question sufficient to support jurisdiction on this ground in federal court.

The same rule applies to chapter headings designating sub-areas within the subjects. They tip you off as to what the text is designed to teach. The cases are arranged in a casebook to show a progression or development of the law, so that the preceding cases may also help.

It is also most important to remember to *read the notes and questions* at the end of a case to determine what the editors wanted you to have gleaned from it.

HOLDING AND DECISION: This section should succinctly explain the rationale of the court in arriving at its decision. In capsulizing the "reasoning" of the court, it should always include an application of the general rule or rules of law to the specific facts of the case. Hidden justifications come to light in this entry: the reasons for the state of the law, the public policies, the biases and prejudices, those considerations that influence the justices' thinking and, ultimately, the outcome of the case. At the end, there should be a short indication of the disposition or procedural resolution of the case (e.g., "Decision of the trial court for Mr. Smith (P) reversed").

The foregoing format is designed to help you "digest" the reams of case material with which you will be faced in your law school career. Once mastered by practice, it will place at your fingertips the information the authors of your casebooks have sought to impart to you in case-by-case illustration and analysis.

B. Be as Economical as Possible in Briefing Cases

Once armed with a format that encourages succinctness, it is as important to be economical with regard to the time spent on the actual reading of the case as it is to be economical in the writing of the brief itself. This does not mean "skimming" a case. Rather, it means reading the case with an "eye" trained to recognize into which "section" of your brief a particular passage or line fits and having a system for quickly and precisely marking the case so that the passages fitting any one particular part of the brief can be easily identified and brought together in a concise and accurate manner when the brief is actually written.

It is of no use to simply repeat everything in the opinion of the court; record only enough information to trigger your recollection of what the court said. Nevertheless, an accurate statement of the "law of the case," i.e., the legal principle applied to the facts, is absolutely essential to class preparation and to learning the law under the case method.

To that end, it is important to develop a "shorthand" that you can use to make marginal notations. These notations will tell you at a glance in which section of the brief you will be placing that particular passage or portion of the opinion.

Some students prefer to underline all the salient portions of the opinion (with a pencil or colored underliner marker), making marginal notations as they go along. Others prefer the color-coded method of underlining, utilizing different colors of markers to underline the salient portions of the case, each separate color being used to represent a different section of the brief. For example, blue underlining could be used for passages relating to the rule of law, yellow for those relating to the issue, and green for those relating to the holding and decision, etc. While it has its advocates, the color-coded method can be confusing and time-consuming (all that time spent on changing colored markers). Furthermore, it can interfere with the continuity and concentration many students deem essential to the reading of a case for maximum comprehension. In the end, however, it is a matter of personal preference and style. Just remember, whatever method you use, underlining must be used sparingly or its value is lost.

If you take the marginal notation route, an efficient and easy method is to go along underlining the key portions of the case and placing in the margin alongside them the following "markers" to indicate where a particular passage or line "belongs" in the brief you will write:

N	(NATURE OF CASE)
RL	(RULE OF LAW)
I	(ISSUE)
HL	(HOLDING AND DECISION, relates to the RULE OF LAW behind the decision)
HR	(HOLDING AND DECISION, gives the RATIONALE or reasoning behind the decision)
HA	(HOLDING AND DECISION, APPLIES the general principle(s) of law to the facts of the case to arrive at the decision)

Remember that a particular passage may well contain information necessary to more than one part of your brief, in which case you simply note that in the margin. If you are using the color-coded underlining method instead of marginal notation, simply make asterisks or checks in the margin next to the passage in question in the colors that indicate the additional sections of the brief where it might be utilized.

The economy of utilizing "shorthand" in marking cases for briefing can be maintained in the actual brief writing process itself by utilizing "law student shorthand" within the brief. There are many commonly used words and phrases for which abbreviations can be substituted in your briefs (and in your class notes also). You can develop abbreviations that are personal to you and which will save you a lot of time. A reference list of briefing abbreviations can be found on page xii of this book.

C. Use Both the Briefing Process and the Brief as a Learning Tool

Now that you have a format and the tools for briefing cases efficiently, the most important thing is to make the time spent in briefing profitable to you and to make the most advantageous use of the briefs you create. Of course, the briefs are invaluable for classroom reference when you are called upon to explain or analyze a particular case. However, they are also useful in reviewing for exams. A quick glance at the fact summary should bring the case to mind, and a rereading of the rule of law should enable you to go over the underlying legal concept in your mind, how it was applied in that particular case, and how it might apply in other factual settings.

As to the value to be derived from engaging in the briefing process itself, there is an immediate benefit that arises from being forced to sift through the essential facts and reasoning from the court's opinion and to succinctly express them in your own words in your brief. The process ensures that you understand the case and the point that it illustrates, and that means you will be ready to absorb further analysis and information brought forth in class. It also ensures you will have something to say when called upon in class. The briefing process helps develop a mental agility for getting to the *gist* of a case and for identifying, expounding on, and applying the legal concepts and issues found there. The briefing process is the mental process on which you must rely in taking law school examinations; it is also the mental process upon which a lawyer relies in serving his clients and in making his living.

Abbreviations for Briefs

acceptance	acp
affirmed	aff
answer	ans
assumption of risk	a/r
attorney	atty
beyond a reasonable doubt	b/r/d
bona fide purchaser	BFP
breach of contract	br/k
cause of action	c/a
common law	c/l
Constitution	Con
constitutional	con
contract	K
contributory negligence	c/n
cross	x
cross-complaint	x/c
cross-examination	x/ex
cruel and unusual punishment	c/u/p
defendant	D
dismissed	dis
double jeopardy	d/j
due process	d/p
equal protection	e/p
equity	eq
evidence	ev
exclude	exc
exclusionary rule	exc/r
felony	f/n
freedom of speech	f/s
good faith	g/f
habeas corpus	h/c
hearsay	hr
husband	H
injunction	inj
in loco parentis	ILP
inter vivos	I/v
joint tenancy	j/t
judgment	judgt
jurisdiction	jur
last clear chance	LCC
long-arm statute	LAS
majority view	maj
meeting of minds	MOM
minority view	min
Miranda rule	Mir/r
Miranda warnings	Mir/w
negligence	neg
notice	ntc
nuisance	nus
obligation	ob
obscene	obs
offer	O
offeree	OE
offeror	OR
ordinance	ord
pain and suffering	p/s
parol evidence	p/e
plaintiff	P
prima facie	p/f
probable cause	p/c
proximate cause	px/c
real property	r/p
reasonable doubt	r/d
reasonable man	r/m
rebuttable presumption	rb/p
remanded	rem
res ipsa loquitur	RIL
respondeat superior	r/s
Restatement	RS
reversed	rev
Rule Against Perpetuities	RAP
search and seizure	s/s
search warrant	s/w
self-defense	s/d
specific performance	s/p
statute	S
statute of frauds	S/F
statute of limitations	S/L
summary judgment	s/j
tenancy at will	t/w
tenancy in common	t/c
tenant	t
third party	TP
third party beneficiary	TPB
transferred intent	TI
unconscionable	uncon
unconstitutional	unconst
undue influence	u/e
Uniform Commercial Code	UCC
unilateral	uni
vendee	VE
vendor	VR
versus	v
void for vagueness	VFV
weight of authority	w/a
weight of the evidence	w/e
wife	W
with	w/
within	w/i
without	w/o
without prejudice	w/o/p
wrongful death	wr/d

Table of Cases

CHAPTER 1

Relationship of Law, Lawyers and Ethics

Quick Reference Rules of Law

Spaulding v. Zimmerman

Injured minor (P) v. Tortfeasor (D)

Minn. Sup. Ct., 263 Minn. 346, 116 N.W.2d 704 (1962).

NATURE OF CASE: Appeal from an order vacating a prior order approving a settlement for personal injuries.

FACT SUMMARY: In agreeing to a settlement for injuries sustained in an automobile accident, Spaulding's (P) attorneys did not know he had an aorta aneurysm possibly resulting from the accident; and Zimmerman's (D) attorneys, who did know, did not disclose it to Spaulding (P) or to the court.

RULE OF LAW

While no rule or duty requires defendants to disclose adverse knowledge when the parties are in an adversary position, once they reach an agreement to settle, defendants who fail to disclose run the risk that failure to affirmatively disclose information may form the basis for vacating a settlement.

FACTS: After Spaulding (P), a minor, was severely injured while riding in a car driven by Zimmerman (D), his father brought suit on Spaulding's (P) behalf. While Spaulding's (P) physicians did not discover that he had a life-threatening aorta aneurysm possibly resulting from the accident, a neurologist who examined Spaulding (P) for Zimmerman (D) pointed it out in his report to Zimmerman's (D) attorneys. The parties reached a settlement agreement and submitted it to the court for approval. The aorta aneurysm was never disclosed to the court. When Spaulding (P) had a subsequent checkup, his physician discovered the aneurysm. Spaulding (P) immediately had surgery. No longer a minor child, Spaulding (P) brought this action for additional damages. The court vacated the prior settlement order. Zimmerman (D) appealed.

ISSUE: While no rule or duty requires defendants to disclose adverse knowledge when the parties are in an adversary position, once they reach an agreement to settle, do defendants who fail to disclose run the risk that failure to affirmatively disclose information may form the basis for vacating a settlement?

HOLDING AND DECISION: (Gallagher, J.) Yes. While no rule or duty requires defendants to disclose adverse knowledge when the parties are in an adversary position, once they reach an agreement to settle, defendants who fail to disclose run the risk that failure to affirmatively disclose information may form the basis for vacating a settlement. In vacating the settlement, the lower court found the aneurysm causally related to the accident. A settlement made on behalf of a minor may be vacated where it is shown that in the accident the minor sustained separate and distinct injuries which were not known or considered by the court at the time the settlement was approved. Here, Zimmerman's (D) counsel knew the seriousness of Spaulding's (P) disability but did not disclose it to the court. Therefore, the court did not abuse its discretion in setting aside the prior settlement. Affirmed.

ANALYSIS

No canon of ethics or legal obligation required Zimmerman's (D) attorney to inform Spaulding (P) about the aneurysm or to advise the court about it. In fact, Spaulding's (P) counsel could have obtained the information through use of the available rules of discovery. Had Spaulding (P) not been a minor at the time of the settlement, the lower court declared it would have been justified in denying his motion to vacate, leaving him to whatever remedy he may have had against his doctor and his lawyer. Note, however, that the rule changes in ex-parte proceedings, where a lawyer must inform the tribunal of all material facts (ABA Model Rule 3.3).

Quicknotes

ABUSE OF DISCRETION A determination by an appellate court that a lower court's decision was based on an error of law.

DISCOVERY Pretrial procedure during which one party makes certain information available to the other.

Commonwealth v. Stenhach

State (P) v. Criminal defense attorneys (D)

Pa. Super. Ct., 356 Pa. Super. 5, 514 A.2d 114 (1986).

NATURE OF CASE: Appeal from convictions for hindering prosecution and tampering with evidence.

FACT SUMMARY: After the Stenhachs (D) retained possession of a broken rifle stock from a rifle used by their client, who was being tried for murder, the trial court insisted that they produce the rifle stock, and the Stenhachs (D) were later charged with hindering prosecution and tampering with evidence.

RULE OF LAW

Physical evidence of crime in the possession of a criminal defense attorney is not subject to an attorney-client privilege and must be delivered to the prosecution.

FACTS: While defending Buchanan on a murder charge, attorneys George Stenhach (D) and Walter Stenhach (D) hired an investigator, Weidner, who found the broken rifle stock from the rifle used by Buchanan. The Stenhachs (D) stored it in a desk drawer in their office. When the trial court learned about the rifle stock, the Stenhachs (D) were ordered to produce it. After Buchanan's conviction, the Stenhachs (D) were charged, under state statutes, with hindering prosecution and tampering with evidence. At their trial they argued unsuccessfully that the attorney-client privilege obligated them to retain the rifle stock to protect their client. Following their conviction and sentencing, the Stenhachs (D) appealed, challenging the trial court's interpretation of the statutes and arguing that the statutes were unconstitutionally vague or overbroad as applied to defense attorneys.

ISSUE: Is physical evidence of crime in the possession of a criminal defense attorney subject to a privilege?

HOLDING AND DECISION: (Hester, J.) No. Physical evidence of crime in the possession of a criminal defense attorney is not subject to an attorney-client privilege and must be delivered to the prosecution. A criminal defense attorney in possession of physical evidence incriminating his client may, after a reasonable time for examination, return it to its source if he can do so without hindering the prosecution of another and without altering, destroying, or concealing it or impairing its verity. Otherwise, he must deliver it to the prosecution on his own motion. However, the statutes against hindering prosecution and tampering with evidence are unconstitutionally vague or overbroad as applied to attorneys engaged in the representation of criminal defendants, and hence their enforcement against the Stenhachs (D) was a denial of due process. Accordingly, the appellants are ordered discharged.

ANALYSIS

Model Rule 3.4(a) prohibits a lawyer from "unlawfully" obstructing another party's access to evidence or "unlawfully" altering, destroying, or concealing a document or other material having potential evidentiary value. Statutory definitions of "unlawful" conduct vis-à-vis destruction of evidence vary from state to state. Although a version of Model Rule 3.4(a) was adopted by Pennsylvania after *Stenhach* was decided, the Stenhachs (D) were not disciplined by the Disciplinary Counsel, which cited as mitigating circumstances the prior case law in their favor, the prosecution's (P) inaction, and Buchanan's conviction.

Quicknotes

ATTORNEY-CLIENT PRIVILEGE A doctrine precluding the admission into evidence of confidential communications between an attorney and his client made in the course of obtaining professional assistance.

OVERBROAD That quality or characteristic of a statute, regulation, or order which reaches beyond the problem it was meant to solve causing it to sweep within it activity it cannot legitimately reach.

CHAPTER 2

Conformity

Quick Reference Rules of Law

United States v. Gellene

Federal government (P) v. Attorney convicted of fraud (D)

182 F.3d 578 (7th Cir. 1999).

NATURE OF CASE: Appeal from a criminal fraud conviction.

FACT SUMMARY: When John Gellene (D) was convicted of fraudulently making a false material declaration in a bankruptcy case in violation of federal statute, he argued that although the false statement was in fact made, it was not fraudulent since it was not made with intent to defraud.

RULE OF LAW

Under the federal Bankruptcy Statute, a statement is fraudulent if made with intent to deceive even if not made with intent to defraud.

FACTS: John Gellene (D), an attorney who represented Bucyrus-Erie Company in its Chapter 11 bankruptcy, filed in the bankruptcy court a sworn declaration that was to include all his firm's connections to the debtor, creditors, and any other parties in interest. The declaration failed to list everyone it should have. Gellene (D) was charged with two counts of knowingly and fraudulently making a false material declaration in the bankruptcy case and one count of using a document while under oath, knowing that it contained a false material declaration in violation of federal statute. The jury found Gellene (D) guilty on all three counts, and Gellene (D) appealed.

ISSUE: Under the federal Bankruptcy Statute, is a statement fraudulent if made with intent to deceive even if not made with intent to defraud?

HOLDING AND DECISION: (Ripple, J.) Yes. Under the federal Bankruptcy Statute, a statement is fraudulent if made with intent to deceive even if not made with intent to defraud. This court rejects Gellene's (D) argument that to commit bankruptcy fraud the defendant must have a specific intent to alter or to impact the distribution of a debtor's assets and not merely to impact the integrity of the legal system, as the government argued. This court cannot accept Gellene's (D) narrowly circumscribed definition of "intent to defraud" or "fraudulently." The plain wording of the statute punishes making a false statement "knowingly and fraudulently." The common understanding of the term "fraudulently" includes the intent to deceive. The expansive scope of the statute reaches beyond the wrongful sequestration of a debtor's property and also encompasses the knowing and fraudulent making of false oaths or declarations in the context of a bankruptcy proceeding. Here, Gellene (D) does not deny that the applications were sworn declarations in a bankruptcy case which were false and knowingly made. The omission of material information in a bankruptcy filing, as here, impedes a bankruptcy court's fulfilling of its responsibilities just as much as an explicitly false statement. Thus, whether the deception at issue is aimed at thwarting the bankruptcy court or the parties to the bankruptcy, the fraud provision of the statute is designed to protect the integrity of the administration of a bankruptcy case. Gellene's (D) failure to divulge his representation of a major secured creditor of the debtor was highly material. Furthermore, the government established Gellene's (D) knowledge of his statutory duty to disclose. Affirmed.

ANALYSIS

As the *Gellene* decision makes clear, materiality in the context of the bankruptcy statute does not require harm to or adverse reliance by a creditor, nor does it require a realization of a gain by the defendant. Rather, it requires that the false oath or account relate to some significant aspect of the bankruptcy case or proceeding. There is no doubt whatsoever that a misstatement in a bankruptcy petition about other affiliations constitutes a material misrepresentation.

Quicknotes

BANKRUPTCY A legal proceeding whereby a debtor, who is unable to pay his debts as they become due, is relieved of his obligation to pay his creditors either by liquidation and distribution of his remaining assets or through reorganization and payment from future income.

FRAUDULENT MISREPRESENTATION A statement or conduct by one party to another that constitutes a false representation of fact.

MATERIALITY Importance; the degree of relevance or necessity to the particular matter.

Arthur Andersen LLP v. United States

Corporation (D) v. Federal government (P)

544 U.S. 696 (2005).

NATURE OF CASE: Appeal from guilty verdict.

FACT SUMMARY: Arthur Andersen LLP (D) was convicted of persuading its employees to destroy documents related to an investigation of Enron Corporation, one of its clients.

RULE OF LAW

A court must find consciousness of wrongdoing when convicting a person under a statute that makes it a crime to "corruptly persuade" another to withhold or alter documents for use in an official proceeding.

FACTS: Arthur Andersen LLP (D) provided accounting services to Enron Corporation. In 2001, an article in *The Wall Street Journal* suggested improprieties at Enron, and the Securities and Exchange Commission (SEC) opened an informal investigation. Arthur Andersen (D) formed an Enron "crisis-response" team, which included in-house counsel Nancy Temple. Less than a month later, one of Arthur Andersen's (D) partners, Michael Odom, held a general training meeting where he urged everyone to comply with Arthur Andersen's (D) document retention policy. This policy called for a single file that "should contain only that information which is relevant to supporting our work" (everything else should be destroyed). In the meeting, Odom stated "If [documents are] destroyed in the course of [the] normal policy and litigation is filed the next day, that's great . . . We've followed our own policy, and whatever there was that might have been of interest to somebody is gone and irretrievable." A week later, the SEC notified Enron that it had opened an investigation and requested certain information and documents. On that same day, Temple sent an e-mail to Arthur Andersen's (D) Enron team reminding them to follow the document policy and attached a copy of it. Several meetings followed, which were all followed by substantial destruction of paper and electronic documents related to Enron. Two weeks later, the SEC served Enron and Arthur Andersen (D) with subpoenas for records, and Arthur Andersen (D) employees were told "No more shredding . . . We have been officially served for our documents." Arthur Andersen (D) was then indicted in the Southern District of Texas for persuading its employees to destroy documents related to the SEC investigation. The district court found Arthur Andersen (D) guilty, and the court of appeals affirmed. The U.S. Supreme Court granted certiorari, focusing on the whether the lower court's jury instructions properly conveyed the elements of a "corrupt[t] persua[sion]" conviction.

ISSUE: Must a court find any consciousness of wrongdoing when convicting a person under a statute that makes it a crime to "corruptly persuade" another to withhold or alter documents for use in an official proceeding?

HOLDING AND DECISION: (Rehnquist, C.J.) Yes. A court must find consciousness of wrongdoing when convicting a person under a statute that makes it a crime to "corruptly persuade" another to withhold or alter documents for use in an official proceeding. Only persons conscious of wrongdoing, can be said to knowingly and corruptly persuade another. Limiting criminality to persuaders conscious of their wrongdoing, complies with the level of culpability usually required in order to impose criminal liability. Importantly, "persuading" a person with the intent to cause that person to withhold documents or testimony from a government proceeding is not inherently wrong. For example, an attorney may persuade a client to withhold documents or testimony, that are subject to, the attorney-client privilege. Reversed and remanded.

ANALYSIS

Although this case does not involve a criminal charge brought directly against an attorney, Temple was a primary player in the case. The government focused on an email Temple sent to Odom that read: "It might be useful to consider reminding the engagement team of our documentation and retention policy. It [would] be helpful to make sure that we have complied with the policy. Let me know if you have any questions." Temple also attached a copy of Arthur Andersen's (D) retention/destruction policy. The head of Enron's engagement team testified he viewed the communications from Temple as encouraging him to destroy documents. Temple argued that her statements were taken out of context. Ultimately, as in other crimes affecting the administration of justice, guilt is determined by the intent of the accused.

Quicknotes

INTENT The state of mind that exists when one's purpose is to commit a criminal act.

SECURITIES AND EXCHANGE COMMISSION Government agency charged with enforcing federal securities law and regulating the United States' stock and options exchanges.

Greycas, Inc. v. Proud

Lender (P) v. Attorney (D)

826 F.2d 1560 (7th Cir. 1987).

NATURE OF CASE: Appeal of award of damages against an attorney under professional liability principles.

FACT SUMMARY: Greycas, Inc. (P) contended that Proud's (D) misrepresentations in his capacity as attorney to Crawford, a party adverse to Greycas (P), were actionable.

RULE OF LAW

An attorney may be professionally liable to one adverse to his client.

FACTS: Crawford was in dire need of capital for his farm business. He approached Greycas, Inc. (P) about a loan, offering his farm machinery as collateral. Upon Greycas's (P) demand, Crawford retained Proud (D), an attorney (and Crawford's brother-in-law), to draft a letter to the effect that he had performed a records search and was satisfied that the machinery had no prior security interests. This Proud (D) did, even though he had in fact conducted no search, and the machinery was subject to a prior security interest. Based on Proud's (D) assertions, Greycas (P) loaned over $1 million to Crawford. The following year, Crawford defaulted and committed suicide. Greycas (P), discovering that it had no security interest of any value, sued Proud (D). A district court, sitting in diversity, entered a judgment of $833,760 in Greycas's (P) favor. Proud (D) appealed, contending he owed no duty to Greycas (P).

ISSUE: May an attorney be professionally liable to one adverse to his client?

HOLDING AND DECISION: (Posner, J.) Yes. An attorney may be professionally liable to one adverse to his client. Courts long ago jettisoned concepts of contractual privity as requirements for liability, replacing them with more general concepts of duty. When the facts of a particular case are sufficient for the finding of such a duty, the adversarial or non-adversarial relationship of the parties is of little matter. In this particular case, Proud (D) made certain misrepresentations to Greycas (P), either intentionally or negligently, or both. The misrepresentations were intended to induce reliance and did in fact induce reliance on the part of Greycas (P), to Greycas's (P) detriment. Whether one considers this to be a case of professional liability or negligent misrepresentation or fraud does not matter. The bottom line is that, under the facts here, Proud (D) owed a duty of care to Greycas (P), which he breached. Affirmed.

CONCURRENCE: (Bauer, C.J.) Proud (D) is clearly liable for fraud, so the discussion of professional liability and negligent misrepresentation was unnecessary.

ANALYSIS

The court here never quite made it clear to the reader whether it reached its conclusion based on professional liability principles or more general principles of misrepresentation. The court essentially admitted this to be the case, but disclaimed any importance thereto. This is not necessarily so, however. Whether the award was based on malpractice or misrepresentation could impact on the availability of insurance indemnification, as well as whether various professional rules of conduct could be implicated.

Quicknotes

FRAUD A false representation of facts with the intent that another will rely on the misrepresentation to his detriment.

MISREPRESENTATION A statement or conduct by one party to another that constitutes a false representation of fact.

PRIVITY Commonality of rights or interests between parties.

SECURITY INTEREST An interest in property that may be sold upon a default in payment of the debt.

CHAPTER 3

Corporate Fraud and Lawyer Action

Quick Reference Rules of Law

In re American Continental Corp./Lincoln Savings and Loan Securities Litigation (Jones Day)

Government (P) v. Bond sellers (D)

794 F. Supp. 1424 (D. Ariz. 1992).

NATURE OF CASE: Memorandum opinion as to the basis of the court's rulings on summary judgment motions in an action for federal securities law violations.

FACT SUMMARY: After Lincoln Savings and Loan (D) failed, five separate actions were filed, with the law firm of Jones Day (D) named as a defendant in four of them due to its activities on behalf of American Continental Corp. (ACC) (D) and Lincoln (D).

RULE OF LAW
Reckless conduct is the highly unreasonable omission involving an extreme departure from the standards of ordinary care, which presents a danger of misleading buyers or sellers that is either known to the defendant or so obvious that the actor must have been aware of it.

FACTS: American Continental Corporation (ACC) (D) retained Jones, Day, Reavis & Pogue (Jones Day) (D) to perform a major internal audit of Lincoln Savings and Loan's (Lincoln) (D) Federal Home Loan Bank Bond (FHLBB) compliance and to help Lincoln (D) deal with the FHLBB's direct investment regulations. Jones Day (D) found multiple regulatory violations. After Lincoln (D) failed, five separate actions were filed, with Jones Day (D) named as a defendant in four of them. Evidence showed that Jones Day (D) instructed ACC (D) in how to rectify deficiencies so that they would not be apparent to FHLBB examiners and that its attorneys participated in creating corporate resolutions to ratify forged and backdated corporate records. The firm also provided an opinion letter in an ACC (D) bond registration statement. Jones Day (D) moved for summary judgment.

ISSUE: Is reckless conduct the highly unreasonable omission involving an extreme departure from the standards of ordinary care, which presents a danger of misleading buyers or sellers that is either known to the defendant or so obvious that the actor must have been aware of it?

HOLDING AND DECISION: (Bilby, J.) Yes. Reckless conduct is the highly unreasonable omission involving an extreme departure from the standards of ordinary care, which presents a danger of misleading buyers or sellers that is either known to the defendant or so obvious that the actor must have been aware of it. The record raises material questions concerning § 10(b), Racketeer Influenced and Corrupt Organizations Act (RICO), Arizona Racketeering Act (AZRAC), common law fraud and deceit, and violations of Cal. Corp. Code §§ 25401 and 25504.1. A question of fact also remains as to whether buyers were injured by the Jones Day (D) opinion letter. Further, Jones Day (D) is an expert under § 11 of the Securities Act, and its advice influenced ACC/Lincoln's (D) conduct. Thus, the order denying summary judgment is affirmed.

ANALYSIS

Attorneys must inform a client in a clear and direct manner when its conduct violates the law. If the conduct continues, the lawyer must withdraw if the representation will result in violation of the rules of professional conduct or other law. Jones Day (D) eventually paid a total of $75 million to settle both the claims of ACC (D) bondholders and stockholders, and the government claims against the firm.

Quicknotes

DECEIT A false statement made ether knowingly or with reckless disregard as to its truth and which is intended to induce the plaintiff to act in reliance thereon to his detriment.

FRAUD A false representation of facts with the intent that another will rely on the misrepresentation to his detriment.

RICO Racketeer Influenced and Corrupt Organization laws; federal and state statutes enacted for the purpose of prosecuting organized crime.

SUMMARY JUDGMENT Judgment rendered by a court in response to a motion by one of the parties, claiming that the lack of a question of material fact in respect to an issue warrants disposition of the issue without consideration by the jury.

Federal Deposit Insurance Corporation v. O'Melveny & Myers

Federal agency (P) v. Law firm (D)

969 F.2d 744 (9th Cir. 1992).

NATURE OF CASE: Appeal from a defense summary judgment.

FACT SUMMARY: When the law firm of O'Melveny & Myers (the Firm) (D) was sued for professional negligence by the Federal Deposit Insurance Corporation (FDIC) (P), as the receiver of a savings and loan association which failed because of the dishonesty of the association's officers, the Firm (D) argued that it had no duty to determine the honesty of its own client.

RULE OF LAW

A lawyer has to act competently to avoid public harm when learning of a dishonest client.

FACTS: The Federal Deposit Insurance Corporation (FDIC) (P), as receiver for the failed savings and loan association American Diversified Savings Banks (ADSB), sued the law firm of O'Melveny & Myers (the Firm) (D) claiming professional negligence in connection with its legal advice and services to ADSB. During the period of the Firm's (D) ADSB representation, officers of ADSB were engaged in fraud and other internal wrongdoings. In its representation of ADSB as to a major real estate development, the Firm (D) failed to communicate with ADSB's accountants or chief financial officer or with federal or state regulators. The FDIC (P) stepped in as conservator for ADSB, having concluded ADSB was insolvent and had incurred substantial dissipation of its assets and earnings due to its violations of state and federal laws and regulations, and its unsound business practices. Subsequently, the FDIC (P) sued the Firm (D), charging it with professional negligence, negligent misrepresentation, and breach of fiduciary duty. The Firm (D) argued that it owed no duty to ADSB to ferret out ADSB's own fraud. The federal district court agreed and granted the Firm's (D) motion for summary judgment. The FDIC (P) appealed.

ISSUE: Does a lawyer have to act competently to avoid public harm when learning of a dishonest client?

HOLDING AND DECISION: (Poole, J.) Yes. A lawyer has to act competently to avoid public harm when learning of a dishonest client. Here, the Firm (D) concedes the existence of a duty by a principal and its agent of complete and accurate disclosure to potential investors in a securities offering. It is an attorney's duty to protect the client in every possible way. Attorneys fulfill this duty by performing the legal services for which they have been engaged with such skill, prudence, and diligence as lawyers of ordinary skill and capacity commonly possess. Furthermore, if an attorney specializes within the profession, the attorney must meet the standards of knowledge and skill of such specialists. An attorney's failure to perform in accordance with such duty is negligence because even as to doubtful matters, an attorney is expected to perform sufficient research. Here, the Firm's (D) attorneys were in fact specialists in securities matters. The Firm (D) is incorrect in its argument that if the client happens to be committing fraud, of which the attorney may or may not be aware, the presence of the fraud cancels the attorney's duty to use due care. Part and parcel of effectively protecting a client, and thus discharging the attorney's duty of care, is to protect the client from the liability which may flow from promulgating a false or misleading offering to investors. An important duty of securities counsel is to make a reasonable, independent investigation to detect and correct false or misleading materials. This, the Firm (D) failed to do. The Firm (D) accordingly failed in its duty to guide ADSB as to its obligations and to protect it against liability. In its "high specialty field," the Firm (D) owed a duty of care not only to the investors, but also to its client, ADSB. Reversed and remanded.

ANALYSIS

As the court made clear in the *O'Melveny & Myers* case, due diligence requires a lawyer's independent investigation of information supplied by an issuer for incorporation into offering materials.

Quicknotes

BREACH OF FIDUCIARY DUTY The failure of a fiduciary to observe the standard of care exercised by professionals of similar education and experience.

NEGLIGENCE Conduct falling below the standard of care that a reasonable person would demonstrate under similar conditions.

PROFESSIONAL NEGLIGENCE The breach of a fiduciary duty owed to one's client, caused by the professional's actions and injurious to the client.

SEC v. National Student Marketing Corp.

Government agency (P) v. Corporation (D)

457 F. Supp. 682 (D.D.C. 1978).

NATURE OF CASE: Civil action seeking injunctive sanctions for aiding and abetting a securities law violation.

FACT SUMMARY: After National Student Marketing Corporation (NSMC) (D) and Interstate National Corporation (D) failed to resolicit shareholders for confirmation of a merger when new information revealed that NSMC's (D) financial statements, showing a profit, were incorrect, the SEC (P) brought suit for injunctive sanctions against the attorneys (D) who participated in the merger.

RULE OF LAW
The three requirements for aiding and abetting liability are a violation of the securities law by the principal, awareness by the defendant that his role was part of an illegal activity, and substantial knowing and assistance in the violation.

FACTS: National Student Marketing Corp. (NSMC) (D), in acquiring Interstate National Corporation (International) (D), prepared a nine-month interim statement, showing a profit. The merger required the issuance of an opinion letter from each corporation's legal representatives and a "comfort letter" from an independent public accountant. Peat Marwick, the accounting firm, found that NSMC's (D) statement had to be adjusted, after which it would show a loss. NSMC's (D) comfort letter, showing the adjustment, was unsigned and not even delivered to the closing meeting until shortly before the filing deadline. However, neither the directors nor the attorneys involved chose to delay the closing to resolicit the shareholders. No effort was ever made to disclose the contents of the comfort letter to Interstate shareholders, the SEC (P), or the public. After a drastic decrease in the price of NSMC (D) stock, the SEC (P) brought an action, seeking injunctive sanctions against NSMC (D) and the representatives (D) of both corporations for securities law violations.

ISSUE: Is aiding and abetting established by a violation of the securities law by the principal, awareness by the defendant that his role was part of an illegal activity, and his knowing and substantial assistance in the violation?

HOLDING AND DECISION: (Parker, J.) Yes. The three requirements for aiding and abetting liability are a violation of the securities law by the principal, awareness by the defendant that his role was part of an illegal activity, and knowing and substantial assistance in the violation. The first element is established by the finding that the principals of Interstate and NSMC (D) committed primary violations of the securities laws. The second element is established because the attorneys (D) for both firms knew that information regarding NSMC's (D) financial status had not been disclosed prior to the merger. Finally, counsel (D) had a duty to the Interstate shareholders to delay the closing of the merger pending disclosure and resolicitation with corrected financials. Their failure to take any action to interfere in the consummation of the merger was a breach of that duty and constituted aiding and abetting, a violation of the antifraud provision. However, the violations seem unlikely to recur, and are insufficient for an injunction.

ANALYSIS

The attorneys (D) violated § 10(b), Rule 10b-5, and § 17(a) of the securities laws through their participation in the closing of the merger. However, the court was confident that the attorneys (D) would take appropriate steps to ensure that their professional conduct in the future comported with the law. The SEC's (P) appeal from this ruling was dismissed when the district court approved a settlement of related private suits against the lawyers (D).

Quicknotes

INJUNCTION A court order requiring a person to do or prohibiting that person from doing, a specific act.

Klein v. Boyd

Investors (P) v. Attorney (D)

Fed. Sec. L. Rep., ¶90,136 (3d Cir. 1998).

NATURE OF CASE: Appeal from summary judgment for defendant in securities fraud case.

FACT SUMMARY: Four investors (P) in a failed limited partnership sued the law firm (D) that represented the partnership for federal securities law violations, common law fraud, and Racketeer Influenced and Corrupt Organizations Act (RICO) violations.

RULE OF LAW

A duty to disclose may arise from either a fiduciary relationship or from affirmative misrepresentations omitting a material fact, and attorneys who significantly participate in the creation of their client's misrepresentations should be held accountable as primary violators under § 10(b) of the Securities Exchange Act of 1934, and Rule 10b-5.

FACTS: Coleman, who had a long history of securities fraud, joined with a new partner to purchase a securities broker business. Drinker (D), an attorney, completed the partnership agreement, a subscription agreement, and a disclosure letter. He also prepared a "November Disclosure Package," which did not contain any information about Coleman's history of fraudulent conduct. When the limited partnership fell into financial difficulties, some investors (P) sued Drinker (D), as well as the partnership (D), for violation of federal securities law, common law fraud, and RICO violations. The district court granted Drinker's (D) motion for summary judgment on all counts, and the investors (P) appealed.

ISSUE: Does an attorney have a duty to disclose if he significantly participates in the creation of his client's affirmative misrepresentation omitting material facts?

HOLDING AND DECISION: (Mansmann, J.) Yes. A duty to disclose may arise from either a fiduciary relationship or from affirmative misrepresentations omitting a material fact, and attorneys who significantly participate in the creation of their client's misrepresentations should be held accountable as primary violators under § 10(b) of the Securities Exchange Act of 1934, and Rule 10b-5. Once a law firm has chosen to speak, it may not omit facts material to its nonconfidential opinions. When a lawyer prepares a document with knowledge that the document will be distributed to investors, the lawyer has elected to speak to the investors, even though the document may not be facially attributed to the lawyer. A trier of fact might reasonably infer that Drinker (D) intentionally concealed material information from the disclosure statements and that he acted with scienter. The judgment of the district court is reversed insofar as it granted the law firm's motion for summary judgment on the federal securities claim and on the investors' common law fraud claim. Since the law firm did not participate in the operation of the purported enterprise, it cannot be liable under RICO laws. Affirmed in part, reversed in part.

ANALYSIS

The court in this case discussed § 10(b) which forbids manipulative or deceptive acts in connection with the purchase or sale of securities. Rule 10b-5 was promulgated by the Securities and Exchange Commission under § 10(b), which makes it unlawful for any person to make any untrue statement of a material fact or to omit to state a material fact which is necessary in order to make the statements made, not misleading.

Quicknotes

FRAUD A false representation of facts with the intent that another will rely on the misrepresentation to his detriment.

MATERIAL FACT A fact without the existence of which a contract would not have been entered.

RICO Racketeer Influenced and Corrupt Organization laws; federal and state statutes enacted for the purpose of prosecuting organized crime.

SCIENTER Knowledge of certain facts; often refers to "guilty knowledge," which implicates liability.

SECURITIES EXCHANGE ACT OF 1934 Federal statute regulating stock exchanges and trading and requiring the disclosure of certain information in relation to securities traded.

In re Refco, Inc. Securities Litigation;

Thomas H. Lee Equity Fund V, L.P. v. Mayer Brown, Rowe & Maw LLP

Investors (P) v. Brokerage law firm (D)

609 F. Supp. 2d 304 (S.D.N.Y. 2009); 612 F. Supp. 2d 267 (S.D.N.Y. 2009).

NATURE OF CASE: Class action seeking damages against law firm for aiding and abetting client's securities law violations.

FACT SUMMARY: Law firm aided client in securities fraud by helping to conceal fraudulent transactions.

RULE OF LAW

Under federal law, there is no private right of action for victims of securities fraud against those who merely, if otherwise substantially and culpably, aid a fraud that is executed by others.

FACTS: Refco, Inc. was among the world's largest providers of brokerage and clearing services in the international derivatives, currency, and futures markets. Refco's business model involved extending credit to its customers so they could make larger trades. Over time, Refco began making loans without adequately assessing customers' credit-worthiness. In the late 1990s, due to several global financial crises, customers suffered huge trading losses and were unable to repay the loans. Instead of disclosing these multi-hundred million dollar losses, Refco hid the losses by essentially making loans to itself through third parties, which would remove the losses from Refco's books at the end of each fiscal period until they were returned just days after the financial period closed. These were referred to as "round-trip loans." Mayer Brown, Rowe & Maw LLP (Mayer Brown) (D) was Refco's outside counsel from 1994 to Refco's collapse in 2005. Mayer Brown (D) was familiar with Refco's operations and finances and participated in 17 rounds of the round-trip loan transactions from 2000 to 2005. Specifically, Mayer Brown (D) explained the structure and terms of the round-trip loans to potential third-party participants, negotiated the loans, and drafted and revised the documentation for the transactions. Mayer Brown (D) later concealed these losses in documents drafted for the Securities and Exchange Commission and for Refco's initial public offering, during which Refco sold approximately one-fifth of its shares to investors. In 2003, Thomas H. Lee Equity Fund V, L.P. (THL) (P) became interested in purchasing an interest in Refco. Mayer Brown (D) was responsible for responding to THL's (P) due diligence requests in connection with the purchase. In doing so, Mayer Brown (D) deliberately concealed the round-trip loans from the fund. In 2004, the fund acquired a majority ownership interest in Refco. In 2005, Refco's losses became public, its stocks plummeted, and it filed for bankruptcy. The fund suffered millions of dollars in losses as a result. Plaintiff investors brought a class action against Mayer Brown (D), claiming damages for Mayer Brown's (D) knowledge and aid regarding Refco's fraudulent actions. THL (P) sued as well, claiming damages under common law fraud for fraudulent statements that Mayer Brown (D) made directly to THL (P). Mayer Brown (D) moved to dismiss all claims under Fed. R. Civ. P. 12(b)(6).

ISSUE: Under federal law, if a client commits securities fraud, is a law firm liable for aiding the client in committing that fraud?

HOLDING AND DECISION: (Lynch J.) No. Under federal law, if a client commits securities fraud, a law firm is not liable for aiding the client in committing that fraud. However, that firm may still be liable under state law covering common law fraud. While the complaint alleged facts that, if true, would make Mayer Brown (D) guilty of aiding and abetting the securities fraud that harmed the plaintiffs, under federal law, there is no private right of action for victims of securities fraud against those who merely—if otherwise substantially and culpably—aid a fraud that is executed by others. Section 10(b) of the Securities Exchange Act of 1934 imposes liability only on a person who makes a false or misleading statement of his own to the plaintiff. Specifically, because § 10(b) only imposes liability for reliance upon a misrepresentation, the misrepresentation had to be directly attributable to the defendant. Anything short of that conduct was merely aiding and abetting, no matter how substantial that aid might be. This requirement draws a "bright line" between the conduct of a secondary actor and that of a primary violator. Ultimately, the plaintiffs were relying on statements made by Refco and passed along or repeated by Mayer Brown (D), not statements made by Mayer Brown (D) itself.

ANALYSIS

While other professional ethics cases and criminal law in general focuses on a defendant's intent, this case largely ignored the issue of intent in favor of a bright-line rule separating secondary actors from the primary violator of the Securities Exchange Act. Other courts, most notably in *In re Enron*, 235 F. Supp. 2d 549 (S.D. Tex. 2002), have found a firm liable as a primary violator when it was consciously and deeply involved in the securities fraud undertaken by its client.

Quicknotes

BRIGHT-LINE RULE A legal rule of decision to help resolve ambiguous issues simply and in a straight-forward manner, sometimes sacrificing equity for certainty.

CHAPTER 4

Confidentiality

Quick Reference Rules of Law

Upjohn v. United States

Pharmaceutical company (D) v. Federal government (P)

449 U.S. 383 (1981).

NATURE OF CASE: Writ of certiorari from order of disclosure of documents in proceedings to enforce tax summonses.

FACT SUMMARY: The Internal Revenue Service (IRS) (P) served summonses on Upjohn (D) that required production both of questionnaires filled out by Upjohn (D) employees at the request of Upjohn's (D) in-house counsel and of Upjohn's (D) counsel's notes of interviews of individuals who had responded to the questionnaire.

RULE OF LAW

Communications by corporate employees to in-house counsel about matters within the scope of the employee's corporate duties are protected from compelled disclosure by the attorney-client privilege.

FACTS: Upjohn (D), a manufacturer and seller of pharmaceuticals, learned during an audit of one of its foreign subsidiaries that certain payments had been made to foreign government officials in order to secure government business. Upjohn (D) decided to conduct an internal investigation. As part of this investigation, Upjohn (D) attorneys prepared a letter containing a questionnaire which was sent to all of Upjohn's (D) foreign "managers." This letter indicated that Upjohn's (D) chairman of the board had asked its general counsel to investigate the existence, nature, and magnitude of any payments made by Upjohn (D) to any employee or official of a foreign government. Managers were instructed to keep the investigation confidential and discuss it only with other Upjohn (D) employees on a "need-to-know" basis; responses to the questionnaire were to be sent directly to Upjohn's (D) general counsel. As part of the investigation, counsel interviewed the questionnaire recipients as well as other Upjohn (D) employees. After Upjohn (D) filed an 8-K with the SEC detailing certain questionable payments, a copy of which was sent to the IRS (P), special agents for the IRS (P) began an investigation into the tax consequences of the payments. As part of the IRS (P) investigation, the IRS (P) issued and served a summons on Upjohn (D) that required production of all files relative to Upjohn's (D) internal investigation. Upjohn (D) refused to produce its questionnaires and responses, as well as its counsel's notes and memoranda of their interviews, on the bases of the attorney-client and work product privileges. The district court agreed with Upjohn (D) and denied enforcement of the summons. However, the court of appeals reversed on the grounds that the work product privilege was never available in tax enforcement proceedings and that the attorney-client privilege extended only to communications between corporate counsel and the corporation's "control group." The U.S. Supreme Court issued a writ of certiorari.

ISSUE: Are communications by corporate employees to in-house counsel about matters within the scope of the employees' corporate duties protected from compelled disclosure by the attorney-client privilege?

HOLDING AND DECISION: (Rehnquist, J.) Yes. Communications by corporate employees to in-house counsel about matters within the scope of the employees' corporate duties are protected from disclosure by the attorney-client privilege. The purpose of the attorney-client privilege is to encourage full and frank communication between attorneys and their clients. The protection of the privilege does not apply only to communications between in-house counsel and a corporation's "control group." Rather, it exists to protect not only the giving of professional advice to those who can act on it but also the giving of information to the lawyer to enable him to give sound and informed advice. Here, information was provided by Upjohn (D) employees to Upjohn's (D) in-house counsel so that they could formulate legal advice concerning compliance with securities and tax laws, foreign laws, currency regulations, duties to shareholders, and potential litigation. These communications are thus protected against compelled disclosure by the attorney-client privilege. Further, Upjohn's (D) notes and memoranda of its counsel's meetings with employees about the foreign payoffs were also protected by the attorney work product doctrine. Under Federal Rule of Civil Procedure 26, the work product doctrine prohibits disclosure, without a strong showing of necessity and unavailability, of the mental impressions, conclusions, and opinions or legal theories of attorneys. Here, Upjohn's (D) counsel's notes did contain its impressions and conclusions, and the IRS (P) could not demonstrate sufficient necessity to overcome the privilege because it remained free to interview Upjohn (D) employees itself and to obtain the same facts Upjohn's (D) attorneys had recorded in their writings. Reversed and remanded.

CONCURRENCE: (Burger, C.J.) The Court should make clear that, as a general rule, a communication is privileged at least when, as here, an employee or former employee speaks at the direction of the management with an attorney regarding conduct within the scope of employment. This Court should articulate a standard to govern similar cases and afford guidance to corporations, counsel advising them, and federal courts.

ANALYSIS

The attorney-client privilege exists not only to protect the giving of professional advice but also the giving of information to the lawyer to enable her to give sound and informed

Continued on next page.

advice. In the case of an individual client, the provider of information and the person who acts on the lawyer's advice are the same person. In the corporate context, however, it can be employees at all levels who could have relevant information needed by corporate counsel if she is to adequately advise the client. These communications must be protected against compelled disclosure in order to satisfy the underlying purposes of the attorney-client privilege. In this case, counsel's notes are also protected by the work product doctrine, Federal Rule of Procedure 26.

Quicknotes

ATTORNEY WORK PRODUCT DOCTRINE A doctrine excluding from discovery work performed by an attorney in preparation of litigation.

ATTORNEY-CLIENT PRIVILEGE A doctrine precluding the admission into evidence of confidential communications between an attorney and his client made in the course of obtaining professional assistance.

United States v. Chen

Federal government (P) v. Importer (D)

99 F.3d 1495 (9th Cir. 1996).

NATURE OF CASE: Appeal from denial of motions to quash subpoenas.

FACT SUMMARY: Chen (D), an importer of goods from Asia, was allegedly engaged in tax fraud through his corporation Sunrider Corporation and TF Chen Products, Inc. The Government (P) sought to prosecute Chen (D) using information and affidavits from Chen's (D) sister and former Sunrider comptroller. The Government (P) also sought the testimony of Chen's (D) attorneys based on the crime-fraud exception to the attorney-client privilege.

RULE OF LAW

The crime-fraud exception applies to the attorney-client privilege even where the attorney is innocent of wrongdoing or guilty knowledge.

FACTS: Chen (D) owns Sunrider Corporation and operates TF Chen Products, Inc., a Sunrider subsidiary. Sunrider imported goods from Asia and paid tariffs on the actual cost of the goods. Sunrider's comptroller, Jau Hwa (Chen's sister), then prepared false invoices on a Hong Kong affiliate's letterhead showing the goods costing much more than they actually did. Sunrider paid income tax on the profit, which was the difference between the sale price of the goods and the fake costs. Chen (D) became concerned that the Internal Revenue Service (IRS) and U.S. Customs would communicate and learn about the difference in the cost of the goods shown on the tariff invoices versus the fake invoices. Customs permits importers to disclose underpaid tariffs before Customs independently learns of the underpayments without penalty or interest. Chen (D) consulted with his attorneys and was advised to file a Customs disclosure. This disclosure was actually a fraud because Sunrider was not underpaying the tariffs but not paying appropriate income tax. The attorneys were not aware of the alleged income tax evasion scheme. Jau Hwa left Sunrider and took several incriminating documents to the Government (P). She also informed the authorities about the alleged tax evasion scheme. The Government (P) indicted Chen (D) for conspiracy, tax evasion, and other crimes. The Government (P) subpoenaed Chen's (D) attorneys to testify about the disclosure statement and their knowledge of the fraudulent scheme, but the attorneys moved to quash based on attorney-client privilege. The trial judge denied the motion based on the crime-fraud exception to the attorney-client privilege so long as the testimony was limited even though the judge did not find evidence the attorneys knew of the alleged scheme. The attorneys appealed.

ISSUE: Does the crime-fraud exception apply to the attorney-client privilege where the attorney is innocent of wrongdoing or guilty knowledge?

HOLDING AND DECISION: (Kleinfeld, J.) Yes. The crime-fraud exception applies to the attorney-client privilege even where the attorney is innocent of wrongdoing or guilty knowledge. Clients will be frightened to tell their attorneys about the entirety of their actions if the attorneys can be forced to become government informants. The attorney-client privilege is crucial to full representation. That privilege cannot, however, shield clients from ongoing or future criminal conduct. The Government (P) here argues the privilege does not apply when the attorneys are acting as "spokespersons" for a company, Sunrider, rather than legal advisors. The attorneys here were not spokespersons such as public relations persons but were lawyers communicating their clients' desires to the court and other authorities. Not all communications are privileged, such as when the attorney does not provide legal advice, but the rebuttable presumption exists when the attorney is retained to give legal advice. Here, Chen (D) retained the attorneys to provide advice about the Customs disclosure. Further, contrary to the Government's (P) argument, Hwa had no authority to waive the attorney-client privilege held by Sunrider because she was an ex-employee and was not given authority by any current officers or management. The Government (P) then has to demonstrate the crime-fraud exception applies without Hwa's information or affidavit. The Government (P) must show a factual basis to support a good-faith belief that an in camera review of the evidence will show that the crime-fraud exception applies. Then the judge may accept in camera review. The Government (P) skipped these steps and submitted Hwa's evidence to the judge. Even absent Hwa's evidence, though, the Government (P) can make out a prima facie case that the crime-fraud exception applies. The facts outside of Hwa's disclosure of confidential information would lead a reasonable person to believe Chen (D) may have sought legal counsel for the furtherance of a crime. The attorneys here were innocent of the tax evasion scheme and had no knowledge of wrongdoing, but the client knew and the attorney-client privilege is the client's. The client waived the privilege. Affirmed.

ANALYSIS

The attorney-client privilege belongs to the client to affirm or waive. When a client engages in wrongful or deceitful conduct, he has implicitly waived that trust relationship with the attorney. Just as when a client threatens harm to a third party, a deceitful client has waived his right to confidentiality any longer. The attorney may not have an affirmative duty to inform authorities as in the threat of a harm situation, but the attorneys cannot withhold the

Continued on next page.

criminal information based on the privilege when confronted with the client's wrongdoing.

Quicknotes

AFFIDAVIT A declaration of facts written and affirmed before a witness.

ATTORNEY-CLIENT PRIVILEGE A doctrine precluding the admission into evidence of confidential communications between an attorney and his client made in the course of obtaining professional assistance.

PRIMA FACIE CASE An action where the plaintiff introduces sufficient evidence to submit the issue to the judge or jury for determination.

QUASH To vacate, annul, void.

SUBPOENA A command issued by court to compel a witness to appear at trial.

In re Columbia/HCA Healthcare Corp. Billing Practices Litigation

Defrauded private payors (P) v. Healthcare provider (D)

293 F.3d 289 (6th Cir. 2002).

NATURE OF CASE: Appeal from a district court order compelling the production of certain otherwise privileged documents.

FACT SUMMARY: When the district court held that Columbia/HCA (D) had waived any attorney-client privilege associated with documents which it had voluntarily disclosed to the Department of Justice during an investigation, Columbia/HCA (D) argued that it had only selectively waived its privilege and had not waived the privilege as to third parties.

RULE OF LAW

The attorney-client privilege is waived en toto by voluntary disclosure of private communications by an individual or corporation to third parties and by other conduct which implies a waiver of the privilege or consent to disclosure.

FACTS: During a Department of Justice (DOJ) investigation of Columbia/HCA (D) for possible Medicare and Medicaid fraud, Columbia/HCA (D), either in response to the investigation or in anticipation of it, conducted several internal audits which examined various billing codes assigned to patients to determine any possible miscoding, deliberate or otherwise, of the patients. After negotiations with the DOJ concerning the fraud investigation, Columbia/HCA (D) agreed to produce some of the coding audits and related documents to the DOJ. In exchange, the DOJ agreed that certain confidentiality provisions would govern its obtaining the documents. Ultimately, the DOJ and Columbia/HCA (D) reached a settlement of the fraud investigation. Once the nature, extent, and results of the DOJ investigation came to light, private insurance companies and private individuals filed numerous lawsuits seeking recovery of excess sums tendered by the private payors (P) to Columbia/HCA (D). The private payors (P) sought an order from the district court compelling Columbia/HCA (D) to produce the coding audits, which the latter refused to do on the grounds of the attorney-client privilege. The district court concluded that Columbia/HCA (D) had waived any privilege associated with the documents, and the latter appealed.

ISSUE: Is the attorney-client privilege waived en toto by voluntary disclosure of private communications by an individual or corporation to third parties and by other conduct which implies a waiver of the privilege or consent to disclosure?

HOLDING AND DECISION: (Russell, J.) Yes. The attorney-client privilege is waived en toto by voluntary disclosure of private communications by an individual or corporation to third parties and by other conduct which implies a waiver of the privilege or consent to disclosure. This court rejects the concept of selective waiver in any of its various forms because such concept has little, if any, relation to fostering frank communication between a client and his or her attorney. It merely encourages voluntary disclosure to government agencies. The attorney-client privilege was never designed to protect conversations between a client and the Government, i.e., an adverse party. Nowhere among the reasons for the privilege is the ability to talk candidly with the government. Secondly, any form of selective waiver, even that which stems from a confidentiality agreement, transforms the attorney-client privilege into merely another brush on the attorney's palette, utilized and manipulated to gain tactical or strategic advantage. Moreover, attorney-client privilege is a matter of common law right. It is not a creature of contract, arranged between parties to suit the whim of the moment. Permitting selective privilege does not serve the public ends of adequate representation that the attorney-privilege is designed to protect. To maintain the all or nothing waiver rule makes the law more predictable and certainly eases its administration. Following a selective waiver approach, on the other hand, would require, at the very least, a new set of difficult line-drawing exercises that would consume time and increase uncertainty. Affirmed.

DISSENT: (Boggs, J.) The court's opinion unnecessarily raises the cost of cooperating with a government investigation. Realistically speaking, the choice before the court today is not between narrower and wider disclosure, but between a disclosure only to government officials and no disclosure at all. A third-party waiver rule would increase the information available over that produced by the court's rule and would aid the truth-seeking process.

ANALYSIS

As the *Columbia/HCA* decision makes clear, once the privacy for the sake of which the privilege was created is gone by the client's own consent, the privilege does not remain for the mere sake of giving the client an additional weapon to use or not at his or her choice.

Quicknotes

ATTORNEY WORK PRODUCT DOCTRINE A doctrine excluding from discovery work performed by an attorney in preparation of litigation.

ATTORNEY-CLIENT PRIVILEGE A doctrine precluding the admission into evidence of confidential communications between an attorney and his client made in the course of obtaining professional assistance.

Meyerhofer v. Empire Fire and Marine Ins. Co.

Investor (P) v. Corporation (D)

497 F.2d 1190 (2d Cir. 1974).

NATURE OF CASE: Appeal from the dismissal of a class action for violation of the Securities Exchange Act and common law negligence, fraud, and deceit.

FACT SUMMARY: After attorney Goldberg (D) was charged with making materially false and misleading statements in connection with a registration statement related to a public offering by Empire Fire and Marine Ins. Co. (Empire) (D), he gave investor Meyerhofer's (P) counsel a copy of an affidavit containing confidential information received from Goldberg's (D) former client, Empire (D).

RULE OF LAW

A lawyer may reveal confidences or secrets necessary to defend himself against an accusation of wrongful conduct.

FACTS: In making a public offering of stock, Empire Fire and Marine Insurance Company (Empire) (D) was represented by Sitomer, Sitomer & Porges (D). Goldberg (D) was an attorney in the firm and had done some work on the issue. Meyerhofer (P) and Federman (P), purchasers of Empire stock, sustained losses when the market price of the stock dropped. They brought a class action suit against Empire (D), alleging, among other things, failure to disclose a large finder's fee arrangement with Sitomer (D). Bernson, Hoeniger, Freitag & Abbey represented Meyerhofer (P) and Federman (P). Goldberg (D) gave Bernson a copy of an affidavit to verify his non-participation in the finder's fee omission. The district court ordered that the Bernson firm and Goldberg (D) be barred from acting as counsel for Meyerhofer (P) in this or any future action against Empire (D) involving the transactions at issue here and then dismissed Meyerhofer's (P) complaint without prejudice. All parties appealed.

ISSUE: May a lawyer, reveal confidences or secrets necessary to defend himself against an accusation of wrongful conduct?

HOLDING AND DECISION: (Moore, J.) Yes. A lawyer may reveal confidences or secrets necessary to defend himself against an accusation of wrongful conduct. In this case, the charge of knowing participation in the filing of a false and misleading registration statement was a serious one. Thus, Goldberg (D) had the right to make an appropriate disclosure about his role in the public offering and to support his version of the facts with suitable evidence. Nevertheless, an attorney may not represent a party in a suit against a former client where there may be the appearance of a possible violation of confidence. Accordingly, the district court's order, prohibiting Goldberg (D) from representing the interests of Meyerhofer (P) and enjoining him from disclosing material information except on discovery or at trial, is affirmed. However, since the Bernson firm's relationship with Goldberg (D) was not tainted by violations of the Code of Professional Responsibility, the order dismissing the action and enjoining Bernson from acting as counsel is reversed.

ANALYSIS

The Model Rule applied here is 1.6(b)(5) and is one of the self-defense exceptions to confidentiality. Comment to Rule 1.6 reveals that the lawyer's right to respond arises when an assertion of complicity has been made. The Model Code of Professional Responsibility does not distinguish between accusations made by a third party and those made by a client.

Quicknotes

AFFIDAVIT A declaration of facts written and affirmed before a witness.

DECEIT A false statement made ether knowingly or with reckless disregard as to its truth and which is intended to induce the plaintiff to act in reliance thereon to his detriment.

DISMISSAL WITHOUT PREJUDICE A final determination of an action without a trial on the merits, allowing the parties from bringing the same action at a later date.

FRAUD A false representation of facts with the intent that another will rely on the misrepresentation to his detriment.

Balla v. Gambro, Inc.

Attorney (P) v. Corporation (D)

Ill. Sup. Ct., 145 Ill. 2d 492, 584 N.E.2d 104 (1991).

NATURE OF CASE: Appeal from reversal of a judgment granting defendant's motion for summary judgment in an action for retaliatory discharge.

FACT SUMMARY: When Balla (P) was discharged from his position as Gambro's (D) in-house counsel after he informed the firm's president that he would take any necessary steps to stop the sale of defective dialyzers, Balla (P) brought this action seeking damages for retaliatory discharge.

RULE OF LAW

In-house counsel should not be allowed the remedy of an action for retaliatory discharge.

FACTS: Balla (P), former in-house counsel for Gambro, Inc. (D), advised Gambro (D) not to accept a shipment of dialyzers from its German affiliate because the dialyzers did not comply with FDA regulations. The dialyzers were to be used by patients with little or no kidney function. At first, Gambro's (D) president informed Gambro Germany (D) that it would not accept the machines, but he later agreed to accept them for sale. Balla (P) informed the president that he would do whatever was necessary to stop the sale of the dialyzers. After Balla (P) was discharged from Gambro's (D) employ, he reported the shipment of the dialyzers to the FDA, which seized them, determining that they did not meet FDA requirements. Balla (P) then sought damages for retaliatory discharge. The trial court granted Gambro's (D) motion for summary judgment. The appellate court reversed. Gambro (D) appealed.

ISSUE: Should in-house counsel be allowed the remedy of an action for retaliatory discharge?

HOLDING AND DECISION: (Clark, J.) No. In-house counsel should not be allowed the remedy of an action for retaliatory discharge. It appears that Gambro (D) discharged Balla (P) in retaliation for his activities, and such discharge was in contravention of a clearly mandated public policy. However, Balla (P) was not just an employee but also general counsel for Gambro (D). Under the Rules of Professional Conduct, a lawyer shall reveal information about a client to the extent it appears necessary to prevent the client from committing an act that would result in death or serious bodily injury. The FDA's seizure of the dialyzers indicates that their use would cause death or serious bodily injury. Thus, Balla (P) was under a mandate to report the sale of the dialyzers. Unlike other employees who are confronted with the dilemma of whether to file for worker's compensation and risk being fired or keep their jobs and lose their right to a remedy, Balla (P) had no choice as to what course of action he could follow. Moreover, extending the tort of retaliatory discharge to in-house counsel would have an undesirable chilling effect on the attorney-client relationship between employers and their in-house counsel. The decision of the trial court is affirmed.

DISSENT: (Freeman, J.) The lawyer's ethical obligation is an inadequate safeguard for protecting the lives and property of Illinois citizens. The incentive needed is recognition of a cause of action for retaliatory discharge. To allow a corporate employer to discharge its in-house counsel without fear of any sanction gives the assistance and protection of the courts to scoundrels. The majority overlooks the very real possibility that discharged in-house counsel will be stigmatized within the legal profession.

ANALYSIS

Generally, a client may discharge his attorney at any time, with or without cause. This rule applies equally to in-house counsel as it does to outside counsel. Employers might be hesitant to turn to their in-house counsel for advice regarding potentially questionable corporate conduct knowing that their in-house counsel could use this information in a retaliatory discharge suit. The Illinois version of the confidentiality rule imposes a mandatory duty of disclosure rather than the permissive rule of disclosure embodied in the ABA Model Rule 1.6(b).

Quicknotes

CHILLING EFFECT Resulting in the inhibition or restriction of an activity.

MANDATORY DISCLOSURE The required communication of certain facts by one party to another.

RETALIATORY DISCHARGE The firing of an employee in retribution for an act committed against the employer's interests.

SUMMARY JUDGMENT Judgment rendered by a court in response to a motion by one of the parties, claiming that the lack of a question of material fact in respect to an issue warrants disposition of the issue without consideration by the jury.

CHAPTER 5

Conflicts of Interest

Quick Reference Rules of Law

Westinghouse Elec. Corp. v. Kerr-McGee Corp.

Nuclear reactor manufacturer (P) v. Oil company (D)

580 F.2d 1311 (7th Cir. 1978).

NATURE OF CASE: Appeal from the denial of a motion by certain defendants to disqualify plaintiff's law firm in an action for restraint of trade.

FACT SUMMARY: After Westinghouse Elec. Corp. (Westinghouse) (P) filed suit against Kerr-McGee (D), Kerr-McGee (D) moved to disqualify Kirkland and Ellis (Kirkland), counsel for Westinghouse (P), due to the simultaneous issuance of a report written by Kirkland on the oil companies, refuting any charge that the oil companies restricted uranium output.

RULE OF LAW

Even where no express attorney-client relationship exists, a fiduciary relationship may result because of the work performed and the circumstances under which confidential information is divulged.

FACTS: Kirkland and Ellis represented Westinghouse Elec. Corp. (Westinghouse) (P) in an antitrust action, alleging restraint of trade in the uranium industry. At the same time, Kirkland produced a report lobbying against the proposed breakup of the oil industry for API, of which Kerr-McGee (D), Gulf (D), and Getty (D) were members. Released the day this suit was filed, the report refuted any charge that oil companies restricted uranium output. Gulf (D), Kerr-McGee (D), and Getty (D), who had provided Kirkland with confidential information for the report, moved to disqualify Kirkland. Using the rules of agency, the district court determined that no attorney-client relationship existed between Kirkland and the oil companies and applied a different imputation of knowledge approach to Kirkland as a large law firm. Gulf (D), Kerr-McGee (D), and Getty (D) appealed.

ISSUE: Even where no express attorney-client relationship exists, may a fiduciary relationship result because of the work performed and the circumstances under which confidential information is divulged?

HOLDING AND DECISION: (Sprecher, J.) Yes. Even where no express attorney-client relationship exists, a fiduciary relationship may result because of the work performed and the circumstances under which confidential information is divulged. Gulf (D), Kerr-McGee (D), and Getty (D) each entertained a reasonable belief that it was submitting confidential information on its involvement in the uranium industry to a law firm that was acting in their undivided interest. These oil companies (D) were not aware of the complaint that Kirkland was filing on behalf of Westinghouse (P). Moreover, the screen Kirkland constructed between the attorneys who wrote the report on the oil companies and those representing Westinghouse (P) was not effective, and that does not modify the presumption that actual knowledge of one or more lawyers in a firm is imputed to each member of that firm. Thus, the district court erred in its approach.

ANALYSIS

The court of appeals found that the substantially related contrary undertakings by Kirkland outbalanced the client's interest in continuing with its chosen attorney. However, the court believed that Westinghouse (P) should have the option of dismissing Gulf (D), Kerr-McGee (D), and Getty (D) from the action or of discharging Kirkland. Since substitute counsel had represented Westinghouse (P) in the case since February 1978, the impact of any changeover had been somewhat eased.

Quicknotes

FIDUCIARY RELATIONSHIP Person holding a legal obligation to act for the benefit of another.

Fiandaca v. Cunningham

Prison inmates (P) v. State of New Hampshire (D)

827 F.2d 825 (1st Cir. 1987).

NATURE OF CASE: Appeal of injunction issued in action based on alleged equal protection violation.

FACT SUMMARY: A settlement offer made by the State of New Hampshire (D) to a class of plaintiffs was contrary to the interest of another client of the offeree's attorney.

RULE OF LAW

An attorney may not represent two clients when a settlement offer made to one is contrary to the interests of the other.

FACTS: A class of plaintiffs comprised of female inmates of the New Hampshire penitentiary system brought action in which they claimed that they were denied equal protection because male inmates enjoyed superior facilities. They were represented by New Hampshire Legal Assistance (NHLA), a public-interest legal organization. NHLA also represented a class of students at a state school in an unrelated matter. At one point the state (D) offered to convert one of the school buildings into a penitentiary for women. The students represented by NHLA vehemently opposed this, and the convict plaintiffs rejected the offer. A trial ensued, and the district court held that the state penitentiary system denied equal protection to female convicts and ordered that a facility be built. The state (D) appealed, contending that the court should have disqualified NHLA from representing the plaintiff class.

ISSUE: May an attorney represent two clients when a settlement offer made to one is contrary to the interest of the other?

HOLDING AND DECISION: (Coffin, J.) No. An attorney may not represent two clients when a settlement offer made to one is contrary to the interests of the other. Rule 1.7 of New Hampshire's Rules of Professional Conduct prohibits an attorney from representing a client if the representation of that client may be materially limited by the lawyer's responsibilities to another client. Loyalty to a client is materially limited when a lawyer cannot recommend a possible course of action due to loyalty to another client. Thus, when a settlement offer is made and a lawyer owes allegiance to a party opposed to that settlement, that lawyer cannot use his independent judgment in advising the client. At this point a conflict exists. Here, NHLA could not recommend the state's (D) settlement offer because of a duty to another client, and it therefore should have been disqualified. [The court went on to affirm the finding of an equal protection violation, holding it not to have been tainted by the conflict, but ordered a retrial as to the remedy.]

ANALYSIS

It is usually possible for a potential conflict to be waived. This requires (1) a reasonable belief by the attorney that he can zealously represent both interests, and (2) a knowing consent by the affected parties. The court here, however, believed the conflict to be real, not potential.

Quicknotes

EQUAL PROTECTION CLAUSE A constitutional guarantee that no person should be denied the same protection of the laws enjoyed by other persons in like circumstances.

INJUNCTION A court order requiring a person to do or prohibiting that person from doing, a specific act.

Cuyler v. Sullivan

Attorney general (P) v. Convicted murderer (D)

446 U.S. 335 (1980).

NATURE OF CASE: Review of habeas corpus granted subsequent to murder conviction.

FACT SUMMARY: Sullivan (D), convicted of murder, was granted habeas corpus because the court found the possibility of conflict in his representation.

RULE OF LAW

Where a defendant raises no objection at trial to multiple representation, the mere potential of a conflict of interest in representation is not sufficient to invalidate a conviction.

FACTS: Sullivan (D) was accused of murder, along with two accomplices. Sullivan (D) was tried separately, his trial occurring first. He was represented by two attorneys, who also represented the accomplices. His attorneys rested without presenting evidence. Sullivan (D) was convicted. He appealed, contending that a conflict of interest existed as to his representation. The conviction was affirmed. He petitioned for habeas corpus. At a hearing, one attorney testified that the decision not to present a case was due to a weak state case. The other testified that he didn't wish to reveal the testimony of certain witnesses, in view of the upcoming trial of the accomplices. The district court denied habeas corpus, but the court of appeals reversed, holding that since a possibility of conflict existed, Sullivan (D) had been denied effective counsel. The Supreme Court granted review.

ISSUE: Where a defendant raises no objection at trial to multiple representation, is the mere potential of a conflict of interest in representation sufficient to invalidate a conviction?

HOLDING AND DECISION: (Powell, J.) No. Where a defendant raises no objection at trial to multiple representation, the mere potential of a conflict of interest in representation is not sufficient to invalidate a conviction. The potential for a conflict of interest exists in every situation involving multiple representation, so to hold that the mere potential of a conflict is sufficient to invalidate a conviction would end multiple representation. However, in many cases multiple representation actually improves the position of the defendant. In light of this, this Court believes that only an actual conflict, as opposed to a potential conflict, should invalidate a conviction. Prejudice is presumed when a conflict exists, but should not be when one is only possible. Reversed and remanded.

ANALYSIS

No objection was made by Sullivan (D) to multiple representation in the underlying trial. In his habeas corpus petition, Sullivan (D) contended that a court should undertake its own investigation to determine the potential for conflicts. Justices Brennan and Marshall took exception to the Court's ruling in this regard.

Quicknotes

HABEAS CORPUS A proceeding in which a defendant brings a writ to compel a judicial determination of whether he is lawfully being held in custody.

State v. Callahan

State of Kansas (P) v. Attorney (D)

Kan. Sup. Ct., 232 Kan. 136, 652 P.2d 708 (1982).

NATURE OF CASE: Appeal from the recommendation of an indefinite suspension of an attorney for violation of certain disciplinary rules.

FACT SUMMARY: In representing both the buyer and the seller in a real estate sale, attorney Callahan (D) failed to disclose to the seller his ongoing business relationship with the buyer, and only later did he inform the buyer that she held only a promissory note, not a second mortgage on the property.

RULE OF LAW

A lawyer seeking to represent multiple parties in a transaction with adverse interests must obtain the consent of each after full disclosure of all conflicts of interest, actual and potential, and the possible effect of such representation on the exercise of his independent professional judgment.

FACTS: After the seller of Kansas farmland, Fulton, and the buyer, Lygrisse, reached a tentative agreement by phone, Lygrisse suggested that attorney Callahan (D) handle the transaction for both of them. Fulton agreed. Callahan (D) prepared the sale contracts in accordance with the terms provided by Lygrisse, without consulting Fulton. Nor did Callahan (D) disclose to Fulton his ongoing business relationship with Lygrisse. Fulton believed that she held a second mortgage on the property. Not until Lygrisse defaulted on the final yearly payment did Callahan (D) refer Fulton to another attorney and advise her that she held only a promissory note. The Board for Discipline of Attorneys (P) recommended indefinite suspension of Callahan (D) for violation of certain disciplinary rules. Callahan (D) appealed.

ISSUE: Must a lawyer seeking to represent multiple parties in a transaction with adverse interests obtain the consent of each after full disclosure of all conflicts of interest, actual and potential, and the possible effect of such representation on the exercise of his independent professional judgment?

HOLDING AND DECISION: (Per curiam) Yes. A lawyer seeking to represent multiple parties in a transaction with adverse interests must obtain the consent of each after full disclosure of all conflicts of interest, actual and potential, and the possible effect of such representation on the exercise of his independent professional judgment. The disciplinary rules further provide that a lawyer shall not engage in conduct involving dishonesty, fraud, deceit, or misrepresentation. Here, when the Fultons asked Callahan (D) about foreclosure proceedings, he advised them not to foreclose. They were not advised that they had no security interest to foreclose until almost two years after Lygrisse defaulted on the final payment. The Fultons looked to Callahan (D) for aid, and his conduct clearly rose to the level of deceit and dishonesty. Affirmed.

ANALYSIS

The duty of good faith imposed upon an attorney does not always cease immediately upon termination of his employment. It continues as long as the influence created by the relationship continues. However, the full disclosure requirement of DR 5-105(c) of the Model Code and of Rule 1.7 of the Model Rules conflicts with the rules of confidentiality. Common representation will almost certainly be inadequate if one client asks the lawyer not to reveal to the other client information relevant to the common representation. Rule 1.7, Comment 31.

Quicknotes

DECEIT A false statement made ether knowingly or with reckless disregard as to its truth and which is intended to induce the plaintiff to act in reliance thereon to his detriment.

FRAUD A false representation of facts with the intent that another will rely on the misrepresentation to his detriment.

PROMISSORY NOTE A written promise to tender a stated amount of money at a designated time and to a designated person.

Brennan's Inc. v. Brennan's Restaurants, Inc.

Attorney's former client (P) v. Attorney's present clients (D)

590 F.2d 168 (5th Cir. 1979).

NATURE OF CASE: Appeal from the disqualification of attorneys in an underlying action for trademark infringement and unfair competition.

FACT SUMMARY: When the Brennan family split ownership of their businesses between two family groups, each group claimed ownership of the registered trademarks, and in the ensuing lawsuit, Brennan's, Inc. (P) sought to disqualify the attorney who had represented all the family corporations.

RULE OF LAW

A former client seeking to disqualify an attorney who appears on behalf of his adversary need only show that the matters embraced within the pending suit are substantially related to the matters or cause of action wherein the attorney previously represented him.

FACTS: All of the corporate parties were owned and closely held by the Brennan family. Wegmann jointly represented all the family businesses in a successful application for registration of three trademarks. Later, a dispute within the Brennan family was resolved by dividing the stock between two opposing groups. Brennan's, Inc. (P) went to one group, while Brennan's Restaurants (D) went to the other group. Wegmann, electing to represent Brennan's Restaurants (D), severed his connections with Brennan's, Inc. (P). This suit was filed after both groups claimed ownership of the registered trademarks. Wegmann retained Sprung to assist him in the defense of Brennan's Restaurants (D). Brennan's, Inc. (P) moved to disqualify both attorneys. The district court granted the motion. This appeal followed.

ISSUE: Need a former client seeking to disqualify an attorney who appears on behalf of his adversary show only that the matters embraced within the pending suit are substantially related to the matters or cause of action wherein the attorney previously represented him?

HOLDING AND DECISION: (Tjoflat, J.) Yes. A former client seeking to disqualify an attorney who appears on behalf of his adversary need only show that the matters embraced within the pending suit are substantially related to the matters or cause of action wherein the attorney previously represented him. This rule rests upon the presumption that confidences potentially damaging to the client have been disclosed to the attorney during the former period of representation. Because a conflict of interest is readily apparent under these facts, the balance weighs in favor of disqualification for Wegmann. However, the balance weighs against disqualification of Sprung. A presumption of disclosure of confidences in his case is inappropriate. Remanded for a finding of whether Sprung has learned from Wegmann information his former client did not want disclosed to his current clients.

ANALYSIS

The obligation of an attorney not to misuse information acquired during representation serves to vindicate the trust and reliance that clients place in their attorneys. A client would feel wronged if an opponent prevailed against him with the aid of an attorney who formerly represented that client in the same matter. The need to safeguard the attorney-client relationship is not diminished by the fact that the prior representation was joint with the attorney's present client.

Quicknotes

TRADEMARK INFRINGEMENT The unauthorized use of anther's trademark in such a manner as to cause a likelihood of confusion as to the source of the product or service in connect with which it is utilized.

UNFAIR COMPETITION Any dishonest or fraudulent rivalry in trade and commerce, particularly imitation and counterfeiting.

Nemours Foundation v. Gilbane

Hospital building foundation (P) v. General contractor (D)

632 F. Supp. 418 (D. Del. 1986).

NATURE OF CASE: Motion to disqualify counsel for the defendant in a dispute arising out of construction of an addition to a hospital.

FACT SUMMARY: Because one of the attorneys working for defense counsel had previously been employed by a law firm representing a co-party of Nemours Foundation (P), Nemours (P) moved to have both the attorney and the law firm currently employing him disqualified from further representation in this case.

RULE OF LAW

An attorney cannot represent a client whose interests are materially adverse to that of a former client where the attorney might have acquired substantially related material in the prior representation.

FACTS: Bradley, an attorney with Biggs & Battaglia, counsel for Pierce (D), was formerly employed by Berg & Associates. In a lawsuit against Pierce (D), Berg represented Furlow (P), a co-party of Nemours Foundation (Nemours) (P), and was also co-counsel for Nemours (P). Nemours (P) was the architectural firm on the project that generated the underlying lawsuit, Furlow (P) the mechanical engineer, Gilbane (D) the general contractor, and Pierce (D) a subcontractor. Neither Bradley nor Biggs knew of the other's involvement in this litigation. When it was discovered, Bradley and his superiors at Biggs immediately took steps to screen him from any contact with the Pierce (D) litigation. Nemours (P) moved to disqualify both Bradley and Biggs as counsel for Pierce (D) due to Bradley's former association with Berg.

ISSUE: Can an attorney represent a client whose interests are materially adverse to that of a former client where the attorney might have acquired substantially related material in the prior representation?

HOLDING AND DECISION: (Farnan, J.) No. An attorney cannot represent a client whose interests are materially adverse to that of a former client where the attorney might have acquired substantially related material in the prior representation. In this case, Bradley is disqualified because while representing Furlow (P), he reviewed confidential documents of Nemours (P) which must be protected since Nemours (P) must be considered Bradley's "client." Although there was no express attorney-client relationship, a fiduciary obligation existed nevertheless. However, nowhere in presenting its argument did Nemours (P) allege the slightest disadvantage or harm resulting from Biggs's continued representation of Pierce (D). Moreover, Pierce (D) would be considerably prejudiced by the disqualification of Biggs shortly before trial is scheduled to begin. Thus, the motion to disqualify Biggs is denied.

ANALYSIS

The trend among courts now is to rule out an "appearance of impropriety" as the sole basis for disqualification. However, certain objective circumstances, including the timing and physical characteristics of the screening, will in many cases require disqualification of an entire firm. The size of the firm remains an important consideration, as well as the nature of the prior involvement of the tainted attorney and the extensiveness of the screening.

Quicknotes

FIDUCIARY DUTY A legal obligation to act for the benefit of another, including subordinating one's personal interests to that of the other person.

Securities Investor Protection Corp. (SIPC) v. Vigman

Government (P) v. Accused (D)

587 F. Supp. 1358 (C.D. Cal. 1984).

NATURE OF CASE: Motion to disqualify plaintiff's counsel in an underlying action for violation of federal securities and racketeering laws.

FACT SUMMARY: Because Boltz and Hartman, counsel of record for SIPC (P), had participated in similar proceedings against one of the defendants in this matter while they were employed as attorneys by the SEC, Vigman (D) and the others sought to disqualify Boltz and Hartman.

RULE OF LAW

A lawyer shall accept private employment in a matter in which he had substantial responsibility while he was a public employee only when the appropriate government agency consents after consultation.

FACTS: Boltz and Hartman, counsel of record for SIPC (P) in this action and members of the law firm of Rogers & Wells, were both formerly employed by the Securities and Exchange Commission (SEC). While with the SEC, they participated in a 1973 civil action against DCS Financial Corporation (D) for fraudulent manipulation of securities. Bunnington Corp. (D), the company into which DCS (D) merged, a defendant in the instant action, was charged with numerous violations of the anti-manipulative provisions of the Exchange Act and Racketeer Influenced and Corrupt Organizations Act (RICO). Vigman (D), who had also been a defendant in the 1973 action, sought to disqualify Boltz and Hartman, along with Rogers & Wells, from further representing SIPC (P) in this action, on the ground that their continued representation in a matter connected to their government work contravened the ethical standards of the legal profession.

ISSUE: Shall a lawyer accept private employment in a matter in which he had substantial responsibility while he was a public employee only when the appropriate government agency consents after consultation?

HOLDING AND DECISION: (Tashima, J.) Yes. A lawyer shall accept private employment in a matter in which he had substantial responsibility while he was a public employee only when the appropriate government agency consents after consultation. The instant complaint includes the alleged manipulation of the price of DCS (D) stock, the precise subject of the 1973 civil action. Thus, Boltz and Hartman are representing SIPC (P) in connection with a matter the SEC prosecuted in the 1973 action. Because both Boltz and Hartman are representing a private client in connection with a matter in which they participated personally and substantially while employed by the SEC and because the SEC has not consented to their continued representation, they must be disqualified from further representation of SIPC (P) in this action. Since SIPC (P) does not contend that Boltz and Hartman have been screened from participation in this action, Rogers & Wells must also be disqualified.

ANALYSIS

Courts have differed as to whether the somewhat subjective standard of the appearance of impropriety under former Canon 9 and DR 9-101 was an appropriate one to guide the conduct of lawyers. Thus, Model Rule 1.11(a), applied here, sets forth more specifically the circumstances in which concern for public confidence in government demands disqualification of a government lawyer. The concerns addressed, however, remain the same.

Quicknotes

FRAUD A false representation of facts with the intent that another will rely on the misrepresentation to his detriment.

RICO Racketeer Influenced and Corrupt Organization laws; federal and state statutes enacted for the purpose of prosecuting organized crime.

CHAPTER 6

Who Is The Client?

Quick Reference Rules of Law

In re Grand Jury Subpoena

Federal government (P) v. Corporation (D)

274 F.3d 563 (1st Cir. 2001).

NATURE OF CASE: Appeal from denial of motion to quash subpoena duces tecum by intervening former corporate officers and former corporate attorney.

FACT SUMMARY: Officers and outside counsel of a closely held corporation claim individual privilege in communications involving the corporation in their corporate capacities based on a private joint defense agreement.

RULE OF LAW

Individual officers in a corporation may not claim individual attorney-client and work product privileges in communications with corporate counsel regarding the corporation in their corporate capacities.

FACTS: Because of the secrecy of grand jury matters, all persons and corporations involved in this matter were referred to by fictitious names. Oldco pled guilty to conspiracy to defraud the Internal Revenue Service (IRS) and agreed to cooperate with the government's investigation of present and former officers, employees, and customers. As part of this cooperation, Oldco expressly waived applicable attorney-client and work product privileges. Soon thereafter, a federal grand jury issued a subpoena duces tecum to Oldco's parent corporation, Newparent, Inc., for records relating to Oldco. Although Oldco was now owned by Newparent, at the time covered by the investigation, Oldco was a closely held corporation run by Roe and Moe. Lawyer was Oldco's principal outside counsel. These three individuals intervened and filed a motion to quash the subpoena. Lawyer claimed that he represented Oldco, Roe, and Moe jointly under a longstanding joint defense agreement; and this agreement provided that all communications among the three clients were jointly privileged and could not be released without unanimous consent. The district court denied the motion to quash. Roe, Moe, and Lawyer appealed.

ISSUE: May individual officers in a corporation claim individual attorney-client and work product privileges in communications with corporate counsel regarding the corporation in their corporate capacities when the officers and the corporation share a joint defense agreement?

HOLDING AND DECISION: (Selya, J.) No. Individual officers in a corporation may not claim individual attorney-client and work product privileges in communications with corporate counsel regarding the corporation in their corporate capacities even if the officers and corporation share a joint defense agreement. When a federal grand jury subpoena is issued to a corporation seeking a subsidiary's records, an individual privilege in those records exists only to the extent that communications made in a corporate officer's personal capacity are separable from those made in his corporate capacity. Privileges are created by the operation of law, and private agreements cannot enlarge their scope. Since the officers were claiming the privilege based on a joint defense agreement, their claim for privilege could not survive the corporation's waiver of these privileges.

ANALYSIS

When a lawyer represents an entity rather than an individual, there are often questions regarding to whom any professional duties are owed. Individual officers of a corporation may assert an individual privilege in any communications only to the extent that communications regarding individual acts and liabilities are able to be segregated from discussions about the corporation. This makes sense since a corporation is an incorporeal entity and most necessarily communicate with counsel through individuals. Importantly, when representing a corporation, the attorney represents the corporation and not the individual officers, shareholders, or directors. The rule the court applies in this case is the majority rule. Model Rule 1.13(a) states, "A lawyer employed or retained by the organization represents the organization acting through its duly authorized constituents" and goes on to specifically define the duties of these lawyers. Even so, under Model Rule 1.13(g), a lawyer representing an organization may also represent a constituent of that organization, as long as the representation does not create a conflict of interest under Model Rule 1.7. This becomes especially problematic in situations where an attorney has represented an entity for a long time, and might begin to feel greater loyalty to that corporation's constituents than the corporation itself.

Quicknotes

MOTION TO QUASH A request to a judge asking the judge to set aside or nullify an action.

SUBPOENA DUCES TECUM A command to a witness to produce documents.

Yablonski v. United Mine Workers of America

Mine worker (P) v. Union (D)

448 F.2d 1175 (D.C. Cir. 1971).

NATURE OF CASE: Appeal from denial of a motion to disqualify counsel in an action for an accounting and restitution of union funds.

FACT SUMMARY: After Yablonski (P) and other members (P) of the United Mine Workers of America (UMWA) (D) brought an action against the UMWA (D), they moved to disqualify the UMWA's (D) outside counsel, on conflict of interest grounds, from representing the UMWA (D) after the firm withdrew as counsel for three of its highest officers.

RULE OF LAW

Where no visible conflict of interest exists between a corporate defendant and individual defendant officers of the corporation, but where one could arise in the future, counsel must be disqualified from representing either defendant in order to remove even the appearance of conflict.

FACTS: Yablonski (P) and other members (P) of the United Mine Workers of America (UMWA) (D) brought an action against the UMWA (D) and three officers (D) seeking an accounting of funds disbursed by the three named officers (D) and restitution of funds allegedly misappropriated and misspent. The three officers were Boyle (D), president of UMWA (D), Titler (D), vice president, and Owens (D), secretary-treasurer. The regular UMWA (D) outside counsel was representing both the UMWA (D) and the officers (D). Yablonski (P) and the others moved to disqualify the firm. After the firm withdrew from representation of the individual officers, it remained as counsel for the UMWA (D), which the district court sustained as proper. Yablonski (P) and the others appealed.

ISSUE: Where no visible conflict of interest exists between a corporate defendant and individual defendant officers of the corporation, but where one could arise in the future, must counsel be disqualified from representing either defendant to remove even the appearance of conflict?

HOLDING AND DECISION: (Per curiam) Yes. Where no visible conflict of interest exists between a corporate defendant and individual defendant officers of the corporation, but where one could arise in the future, counsel must be disqualified from representing either defendant to remove even the appearance of conflict. Even if the UMWA (D) and its officers (D) correctly stated that no visible conflict of interest exists at the present time, they cannot be sure that such will not arise in the future. Like a stockholder derivative suit, this case is a derivative action for the benefit of the UMWA (D). When stockholders bring a derivative suit, corporate counsel never gets involved; the counsel charged with protecting the corporation's interest must have no personal ties with the incumbent officeholders. This case must be viewed in its relationship to the numerous cases already pending or decided, in which regular counsel has already undertaken the representation of Boyle (D) individually. Thus, the public interest would be much better served by having an unquestionably independent new counsel in this case. Reversed.

ANALYSIS

Note the analogy between this action and a shareholder's derivative suit. In both cases, the plaintiffs bring suit against the corporation/union to enforce certain fiduciary duties on behalf of the corporation/union. At the time of this suit, Yablonski (P) was attempting to wrest control of the UMWA (D) from Boyle (D). Yablonski (P) and his family were later murdered, and Boyle (D), along with others, was convicted of conspiring in Yablonski's (P) murder.

Quicknotes

DERIVATIVE SUIT Action asserted by a shareholder in order to enforce a cause of action on behalf of the corporation.

Fassihi v. Sommers, Schwartz, Silver, Schwartz and Tyler, P.C.

Physician (P) v. Law firm (D)

Mich. Ct. App., 107 Mich. App. 509, 309 N.W.2d 645 (1981).

NATURE OF CASE: Interlocutory appeals from the denial of defendant's motion for summary judgment and plaintiff's motion to compel discovery.

FACT SUMMARY: When 50 percent shareholder Fassihi's (P) membership in a closely held medical corporation was terminated, he filed suit against the corporation's law firm for breach of fiduciary, legal, and ethical duties and for fraud.

RULE OF LAW

Although a law firm for a closely held corporation generally represents the corporation and not its individual shareholders, the law firm may owe a fiduciary duty to a 50 percent shareholder.

FACTS: Doctors Fassihi (P) and Lopez, radiologists and equal shareholders in a professional medical corporation, were also on the staff of St. Mary's Hospital. The law firm of Sommers, Schwartz, Silver, Schwartz and Tyler, P.C. (Sommers) (D) represented the corporation. Sommers (D) never disclosed to Fassihi (P) that it also represented Lopez individually or that Lopez's agreement with the hospital gave him personal and sole responsibility for the radiology department. Approximately eighteen months after they formed the corporation, Lopez arranged to terminate, with Sommers's (D) help, Fassihi's (P) interest in the corporation, at which time the hospital informed Fassihi (P) that he could no longer practice there. In the ensuing lawsuit, Fassihi (P) claimed that Sommers, (D) had represented both Lopez individually and the professional corporation without telling him and that he, Fassihi (P), had an attorney-client relationship that Sommers (D) had breached. The court denied both Sommers's (D) motion for summary judgment and Fassihi's (P) motion to compel discovery when Epstein, an attorney with Sommers (D), claimed attorney-client privilege. The court then granted leave for these interlocutory appeals.

ISSUE: Although a law firm for a closely held corporation generally represents the corporation and not its individual shareholders, may the law firm owe a fiduciary duty to a 50 percent shareholder?

HOLDING AND DECISION: (Per curiam) Yes. Although a law firm for a closely held corporation generally represents the corporation and not its individual shareholders, the law firm may owe a fiduciary duty to a 50 percent shareholder. Because the attorney's client is the corporation, no attorney-client relationship existed between Fassihi (P) and Sommers (D). However, that did not necessarily mean that Sommers (D) had no fiduciary duty to Fassihi (P). Sommers (D) also had an obligation to divulge to Fassihi (P) its dual representation of the corporation and Lopez individually. Sommers (D) had no obligation to divulge the contents of the Lopez–St. Mary's contract since that information arose out of its confidential relationship with Lopez. But, as a member of the board of directors, Fassihi (P) was entitled to any communications concerning his ouster from the corporation, and Sommers (D) may not assert the attorney-client privilege in that matter. Moreover, Fassihi's (P) allegations were sufficient to prevent Sommers (D) from invoking the privilege because the attorney-client privilege does not protect communications made for the purpose of perpetrating a fraud. Motion for summary judgment is denied.

ANALYSIS

When an entity is small, it does not make much sense to conclude that counsel to a corporation whose officers and shareholder consist of only two people "represents the organization acting through its duly authorized constituents," as the Model Rule 1.13(a) directs. Other courts considering the problem have held that such counsel represents the individual shareholders as clients jointly with the closely held corporation. In other words, it is reasonable for a 50 percent shareholder to believe that the corporation's lawyer is in effect his own individual attorney.

Quicknotes

ATTORNEY-CLIENT PRIVILEGE A doctrine precluding the admission into evidence of confidential communications between an attorney and his client made in the course of obtaining professional assistance.

DISCOVERY Pretrial procedure during which one party makes certain information available to the other.

FIDUCIARY DUTY A legal obligation to act for the benefit of another, including subordinating one's personal interests to that of the other person.

FRAUD A false representation of facts with the intent that another will rely on the misrepresentation to his detriment.

PER CURIAM Announcement of a brief decision without a written opinion.

SUMMARY JUDGMENT Judgment rendered by a court in response to a motion by one of the parties, claiming that the lack of a question of material fact in respect to an issue warrants disposition of the issue without consideration by the jury.

Fickett v. Superior Court of Pima County

Attorney (D) v. Court (P)

Ariz. Ct. App., 27 Ariz. App. 793, 558 P.2d 988 (1976).

NATURE OF CASE: Special action challenging the trial court's denial of defendant's motion for summary judgment.

FACT SUMMARY: When a guardian, whom Fickett (D) represented, misappropriated the guardianship estate, converting the funds to his own use, a successor conservator (P) brought suit against Fickett (D) for negligently failing to discover the misappropriation scheme.

RULE OF LAW

Where an attorney undertakes to represent the guardian of an incompetent, he assumes a relationship not only with the guardian but also with the ward.

FACTS: Fickett (D), attorney for the former guardian of an incompetent, elderly woman, did not know his client had schemed to misappropriate the guardianship estate, converting the funds to his own use. When a successor conservator was able to recover only a small amount from the former guardian or third parties, it brought this proceeding against Fickett (D) and the law firm that had represented the former guardian for negligently failing to discover the guardian's misappropriation. Fickett (D) moved for summary judgment, contending that, as a matter of law, since there was no fraud or collusion between the guardian and himself, he was not liable for his client's misappropriation of the guardianship estate. The Superior Court denied the motion. Fickett (D) challenged the ruling by this special action.

ISSUE: Where an attorney undertakes to represent the guardian of an incompetent, does he assume a relationship not only with the guardian but also with the ward?

HOLDING AND DECISION: (Howard, C.J.) Yes. Where an attorney undertakes to represent the guardian of an incompetent, he assumes a relationship not only with the guardian but also with the ward. Liability to a third person is a matter of policy and involves the balancing of various factors, among which are the foreseeability of harm to the plaintiff, the degree of certainty that he suffered injury, the closeness of the connection between the defendant's conduct and the injuries suffered, and the policy of preventing future harm. The public policy of this state permits the imposition of a duty under the circumstances presented here. If Fickett (D) knew or should have known that the guardian was acting adversely to his ward's interest, the possibility of frustrating the whole purpose of the guardianship became foreseeable, as did the possibility of injury to the ward. Thus, the ruling denying Fickett's (D) motion for summary judgment is upheld.

ANALYSIS

The general rule for many years has been that an attorney could not be liable to one other than his client in an action arising out of his professional duties, in the absence of fraud or collusion. The present conservator (P) conceded that no fraud or collusion existed. However, he argued, and the court agreed, that one could not say as a matter of law that Fickett (D) owed no duty to the ward.

Quicknotes

COLLUSION An agreement between two or more parties to engage in unlawful conduct or in other activities with an unlawful goal, typically involving fraud.

CONSERVATOR A court-appointed custodian of property belonging to a person found to be unable to manage his/her property.

FRAUD A false representation of facts with the intent that another will rely on the misrepresentation to his detriment.

GUARDIANSHIP A legal relationship whereby one party is responsible for the care and control over another and his property due to some legal incapacity on the part of the ward.

SUMMARY JUDGMENT Judgment rendered by a court in response to a motion by one of the parties, claiming that the lack of a question of material fact in respect to an issue warrants disposition of the issue without consideration by the jury.

WARD A minor or incompetent who the court determines to be incapable of handling his own affairs and places in the care of a guardian or conservator.

Paradigm Ins. Co. v. Langerman Law Offices

Insurance company (P) v. Law firm (D)

Ariz. Sup. Ct., 24 P.3d 593 (2001).

NATURE OF CASE: Appeal from the reversal of a defense summary judgment.

FACT SUMMARY: When Langerman (D) was sued for legal malpractice by Paradigm Insurance Company (P) which had hired him to defend one of its insureds, Langerman (D) argued that since there was no express agreement that he also represented Paradigm (P), he had no attorney-client relationship with Paradigm (P) on which Paradigm (P) could base its suit.

RULE OF LAW

An express agreement is not a prerequisite to the formation of an attorney-client relationship.

FACTS: Paradigm Insurance Company (P) issued an insurance policy covering a physician for medical malpractice liability. The physician was sued for malpractice, and Paradigm (P) hired an attorney, Langerman (D), to defend the case. Langerman (D) failed to perform certain investigations regarding the case which were vital to a competent defense. Furthermore, Paradigm (P) subsequently learned that Langerman (D) had undertaken representation of a claimant who was bringing an action against another Paradigm-insured physician. The latter representation violated an agreement between Paradigm (P) and Langerman (D) that the latter would not represent any claimants against Paradigm's (P) insureds. Paradigm (P) brought suit against Langerman (D) for malpractice. On summary judgment, the trial judge held that because there was no express agreement that Langerman (D) could represent both Paradigm (P) and the physician whom Paradigm (P) insured, no attorney-client relationship existed between Langerman (D) and Paradigm (P), hence Langerman (D) owed no duty of care to Paradigm (P) and could not be held liable for negligence that injured only Paradigm (P) but not Langerman's (D) sole client, the insured physician. The court of appeals reversed, holding that here there was a dual attorney-client relationship. Langerman (D) appealed.

ISSUE: Is an express agreement a prerequisite to the formation of an attorney-client relationship?

HOLDING AND DECISION: (Feldman, J.) No. An express agreement is not a prerequisite to the formation of an attorney-client relationship. Quite to the contrary, a relationship of client and lawyer arises when a person manifests to a lawyer the person's intent that the lawyer provides legal services for the person and the lawyer manifests to the person consent to do so. Indeed, either intent or acquiescence may establish the relationship. As a practical matter, an attorney is deemed to be dealing with a client, as here, when it may fairly be said that because of other transactions an ordinary person would look to the lawyer as a protector rather than as an adversary. Thus, a purported client's belief that the lawyer was their attorney is crucial to the existence of an attorney-client relationship so long as that belief is objectively reasonable. The instant case presents the typical situation found when defense is provided by a liability insurer as part of the insurer's obligation to provide for the insured's defense, which includes the power to select the lawyer that will defend the claim. However, the fact the lawyer is chosen, assigned, and paid by the insurer for the purpose of representing the insured does not automatically create an attorney-client relationship between the insurer and lawyer. Here, in the absence of a conflict, the attorney, Langerman (D) has two clients, the insurer Paradigm Ins. Co. (P) and the insured. Here, Paradigm Ins. Co. (P) is in some ways dependent upon the lawyer it hired on behalf of its insured. For example, Paradigm Ins. Co. (P) depended on the lawyer to represent the insured zealously so as to honor its contractual agreement to provide the defense when liability allegations were leveled at the insured. In addition, Paradigm Ins. Co. (P) depended on Langerman (D) to thwart claims of liability and, in the event liability was found, to minimize its damages. Thus, Langerman's (D) duties to the insured were discharged for the full or partial benefit of the nonclient Paradigm Ins. Co. (P). Affirmed.

ANALYSIS

As noted in the *Paradigm* decision most jurisdictions which have addressed the issue, permit the lawyer to represent both the insurer and insured in the absence of a conflict of interest, and some jurisdictions regard both the insurer and the insured as clients of the lawyer even absent an express agreement. All jurisdictions recognize that lawyers for the insured owe at least some obligations to the insurer. Neither the Model Rules nor the Restatement takes a position on the question of whom the insurance defense lawyer represents.

Quicknotes

ATTORNEY-CLIENT RELATIONSHIP The confidential relationship established when a lawyer enters into employment with a client.

Georgine v. Amchem Products, Inc.

Class action plaintiffs (P) v. Asbestos manufacturers (D)

157 F.R.D. 246 (E.D. Pa. 1994).

NATURE OF CASE: Review of stipulation of settlement of class action litigation.

FACT SUMMARY: A proposed settlement of a class action suit for asbestos-related injuries or wrongful deaths was reviewed by the court to determine whether to enter a final class certification under Rule 23, and to approve the settlement negotiated on behalf of the class.

RULE OF LAW

The simultaneous representation of present and future claimants by counsel in a class action suit does not constitute an impermissible conflict of interest.

FACTS: A class of persons exposed to the asbestos products of twenty defendant companies filed a complaint, and an answer and a proposed settlement were filed with the court. Some members of the proposed class objected to the certification of the class, claiming they were not adequately represented, and to the fairness of the settlement. The court reviewed the proposed settlement and considered the objectors' allegations of collusion among class counsel.

ISSUE: Does the simultaneous representation of present and future claimants by counsel in a class action suit constitute an impermissible conflict of interest?

HOLDING AND DECISION: (Reed, J.) No. The simultaneous representation of present and future claimants by counsel in a class action suit does not constitute an impermissible conflict of interest. The settlement terms are fair and reasonable to the members of the class. It is not a conflict of interest for a lawyer to represent two groups of clients with similar claims against a common defendant. Class counsels were highly respected for their skills and experience in asbestos litigation, and there was no suggestion in the exhaustive discovery and litigated record that there was any atmosphere of collusion. Both sides bargained vigorously and at arm's-length. The settlement amounts were generally consistent with historical settlement averages for comparable settlements, were not inflated, and were not the product of collusion. Affirmed.

ANALYSIS

The court in this case discussed the inadequacy of the present tort system to deal with such litigation. Costly and time-consuming litigation could be avoided by such settlements. The claim procedures under the settlement are essentially non-adversarial.

Quicknotes

BARGAINING AT ARM'S LENGTH A course of dealing between parties, who are unrelated and are motivated by purely independent interests.

CLASS ACTION SUIT A suit commenced by a representative on behalf of an ascertainable group that is too large to appear in court, who shares a commonality of interests and who will benefit from a successful result.

SETTLEMENT An agreement entered into by the parties to a civil lawsuit agreeing upon the determination of rights and issues between them, thus disposing of the need for judicial determination.

CHAPTER 7

Litigation and Negotiation

Quick Reference Rules of Law

United States v. Shaffer Equipment Co.

Federal government (P) v. Waste spiller (D)

11 F.3d 450 (4th Cir. 1993).

NATURE OF CASE: Appeal from dismissal of case as sanction for attorney breach.

FACT SUMMARY: Attorneys for the United States Environmental Protection Agency (EPA) (P) deliberately concealed the misrepresented achievements and credentials of the EPA (P) On-Site Coordinator responsible for the preparation of the administrative hearing documents. The court sanctioned counsel for the concealment by dismissing the case in its entirety.

RULE OF LAW

Zealous advocacy on behalf of a client may not include misrepresenting material facts to the court or opposing counsel.

FACTS: Robert E. Caron was the On-Site Coordinator for a United States Environmental Protection Agency (EPA) (P) clean-up site. Caron claimed to have a B.S. in environmental science from Rutgers University and an M.S. in organic chemistry from Drexel, but neither university had records of Caron receiving such degrees. J. Jarod Snyder, a Department of Justice attorney, represented the EPA (P), including Caron, at depositions. Snyder was aware that Caron had not received a degree from Rutgers. Caron testified at his deposition about his alleged educational background and Snyder objected to the continued questions as irrelevant but did not reveal the truth about Caron's credentials. When defense counsel suggested obtaining a court ruling on the objection, Snyder requested a recess and contacted his superior, William A. Hutchins. Snyder was advised to inform Caron he may wish to cease answering and seek individual counsel. Caron chose to continue answering and Snyder continued to state objections to the line of questioning about Caron's credentials. Defense counsel argued the questions were relevant because they went to Caron's credibility. Snyder, after research, determined the questions were relevant but still failed to alert defense counsel or withdraw the objections. The Inspector General later opened a criminal investigation into Caron's misrepresentations, but no one alerted the court or defense counsel to the ongoing investigation. Further, Snyder based his motion for summary judgment on Caron's administrative documents although he did not cite to Caron's testimony or include Caron's affidavit. He still did not inform the court or defense counsel of Caron's misrepresented credentials. Hutchens continued to advise Snyder to delete reference to the criminal investigation in correspondence and avoid notification to the court or defense counsel. Defense counsel then independently learned Caron falsely testified in another case and so informed the Assistant United States Attorney. At that time, EPA (P) informed the court and defense counsel of the "Caron problem" and requested a stay. The district court held that Snyder and Hutchins violated their duty of candor to the court and failed to supplement discovery with material information. The court sanctioned counsel by dismissing the action in its entirety and awarding costs to the defendant. EPA (P) appealed.

ISSUE: May zealous advocacy on behalf of a client include misrepresenting material facts to the court or opposing counsel?

HOLDING AND DECISION: (Niemeyer, J.) No. Zealous advocacy on behalf of a client may not include misrepresenting material facts to the court or opposing counsel. Attorneys, as officers of the court, must first ensure the integrity of the judicial system by advancing honesty on behalf of their clients. Here, Rule 3.3 requires candor before the tribunal and Rule 3.4 requires candor to opposing counsel. Snyder and Hutchins violated both rules as well as the general duty of candor and good faith. Rule 3.3 requires "actual knowledge" of a falsehood as well as materiality of that falsehood. EPA (P) argues its counsel had suspicions of Caron's misrepresentations, but that argument rings false when confronted with the extent and repetition of Caron's fraudulent claims. Snyder had direct knowledge that Caron did not have a degree from Rutgers, did not correct Caron's false testimony in his deposition, did not correct Caron's fraudulent employment application with the EPA (P), and relied on Caron's complied administrative record for the summary judgment motion. The EPA (P) certainly had actual knowledge of Caron's lack of credibility. Next, the court must consider whether the falsehoods were material to the case. The EPA (P) had to prove that its costs incurred in cleaning defendant's site were due to defendant's release or threatened release of hazardous waste. The costs occurred because of Caron's recommendations and the administrative record supporting the costs was compiled at Caron's direction. Thus, Caron's credibility was relevant and material to the case. In fact, Snyder discovered the relevancy in his own legal research. The final factor to consider is whether Caron's conduct is a fraudulent act of the EPA (P). It is characterized as such because Caron is an important witness for EPA's (P) case, the EPA (P) covered up his misrepresentations made during his employ with the EPA (P), and did so for the purpose of disguising a weakness in the case. The attorneys placed themselves at risk for sanction in overstepping the bounds of zealous advocacy on behalf of the EPA (P). Dismissal, however, was too severe a sanction.

Continued on next page.

The defendants would benefit to a greater degree than the harm caused by the attorney's breach. The court affirms the existence of a breach but vacates the order of dismissal and remands for imposition of a sanction short of dismissal. Affirmed in part; vacated in part; and remanded.

ANALYSIS

The judicial system relies on the general honesty of its participants. Justice is served when the truth is uncovered and the appropriate parties receive the appropriate relief; whether that is civil relief or criminal punishment. When attorneys participate in putting forth misrepresentations, deceit, or outright lies, the judicial system fails. When an attorney uncovers a discrepancy in a client's story, background, or credentials, the attorney generally has plenty of opportunity to correct the misrepresentation, counsel the client appropriately to avoid further harm, or find a replacement witness/expert/theory. Here, the attorneys let opportunity after opportunity pass them by while they engaged in the client's deceit. This undermines the overall integrity of the system and justice cannot be served.

Quicknotes

BREACH The violation of an obligation imposed pursuant to contract or law, by acting or failing to act.

MOTION FOR SUMMARY JUDGMENT Judgment rendered by a court in response to a motion by one of the parties, claiming that the lack of a question of material fact in respect to an issue warrants disposition of the issue without consideration by the jury.

SANCTIONS A penalty imposed in order to ensure compliance with a statute or regulation.

STAY An order by a court requiring a party to refrain from a specific activity until the happening of an event or upon further action by the court.

Nix v. Whiteside

Iowa attorney general (P) v. Convicted murderer (D)

475 U.S. 157 (1986).

NATURE OF CASE: Review of order granting habeas corpus subsequent to murder conviction.

FACT SUMMARY: Whiteside (D) contended that his counsel's refusal to allow him to commit perjury denied him his right to counsel.

RULE OF LAW

A criminal defendant is not denied the right to counsel if his counsel refuses to allow him to commit perjury.

FACTS: An altercation involving Whiteside (D) resulted in the stabbing death of another. Prior to testifying, Whiteside (D) told his attorney that he intended to state that he had seen a gun in the decedent's hand, even though he had previously stated to the contrary. The attorney informed him that to do so would constitute perjury, which he could not allow. The attorney informed Whiteside (D) that if he did so testify, he would inform the court of Whiteside's (D) perjury. Whiteside (D) did not so testify, and he was convicted of murder. He appealed, contending that counsel's threats to expose his perjury constituted a denial of counsel under the Sixth Amendment. This conviction was affirmed. Whiteside (D) petitioned for habeas corpus in the district court. This was denied. The court of appeals reversed, agreeing with Whiteside's (D) contention. The Supreme Court granted review.

ISSUE: Is a criminal defendant denied the right to counsel if his counsel refuses to allow him to commit perjury?

HOLDING AND DECISION: (Burger, C.J.) No. A criminal defendant is not denied the right to counsel if his counsel refuses to allow him to commit perjury. The Sixth Amendment's right to counsel clause is not abridged unless counsel is so ineffective as not to have been functioning as counsel. It is the duty of the counsel to take all lawful measure to exonerate his client. However, counsel has no right to violate the law or to assist others in doing so. Further, DR 7–102 of the ABA Code of Professional Responsibility prohibits an attorney from knowingly using perjured testimony or false evidence. Since counsel is not permitted to assist in perjury, it can hardly be considered ineffectiveness when he refuses to do so. Here, the only basis for Whiteside's (D) contention regarding ineffectiveness was the refusal to allow him to perjure himself, and therefore no Sixth Amendment violation occurred. Reversed.

CONCURRENCE: (Brennan, J.) The Court has no right to inject its views of ethical conduct into matters of state jurisdiction. The underlying case was state, not federal, so the Court's inquiries into legal ethics were inappropriate.

CONCURRENCE: (Blackmun, J.) Whiteside's (D) argument is that he would have been acquitted had he been allowed to testify falsely. The answer to this is that the prevention of perjury can never be the basis for a conclusion that the trial was unfair, and therefore a defendant can never claim prejudice due to such prevention.

ANALYSIS

It has never been affirmatively held that an accused has an absolute right to testify on his own behalf. In fact, at one time an accused was categorically prohibited from such testimony. While not expressly approving such a right, the Court here simply noted in passing that such a right is universally recognized.

Quicknotes

HABEAS CORPUS A proceeding in which a defendant brings a writ to compel a judicial determination of whether he is lawfully being held in custody.

PERJURY The making of false statements under oath.

SIXTH AMENDMENT Provides the right to a speedy trial by impartial jury, the right to be informed of the accusation, to confront witnesses and to have the assistance of counsel in all criminal prosecutions.

Messing, Rudavsky & Weliky, P.C. v. President and Fellows of Harvard College

Law firm (P) v. College (D)

Mass. Sup. Jud. Ct., 436 Mass. 347, 764 N.E.2d 825 (2002).

NATURE OF CASE: Appeal from a court's sanctioning of a law firm for an ethics code violation.

FACT SUMMARY: When the law firm of Messing, Rudavsky & Weliky (MR & W) (P), after initiating suit against Harvard College (D), communicated ex parte with employees of the latter, the trial court sanctioned the law firm (P) for violating a Massachusetts rule prohibiting an attorney from speaking ex parte to employees of an organization which is an adversary litigant.

RULE OF LAW

An attorney is banned from ex parte contact only with those employees of an adversary organization who have the authority to commit the organization to a position regarding the subject matter of the case.

FACTS: The law firm of Messing, Rudavsky & Weliky (MR & W) (P) filed an employment discrimination complaint against Harvard College (D) on behalf of a woman sergeant with the Harvard University Police Department (HUPD). Following institution of the suit, the law firm (P), in further investigation of its client's case, communicated ex parte with five employees of the HUPD. It was not claimed that any of the five employees were involved in the alleged discrimination or exercised management authority with respect to the alleged discriminatory acts. The trial court granted Harvard's (D) motion to sanction MR & W (P) for violating a Massachusetts rule, adopted from the American Bar Association's Model Rules of Professional Conduct, that essentially prohibits an attorney from speaking ex parte to employees of an organization which is an adversary litigant. MR & W (P) appealed.

ISSUE: Is an attorney banned from ex parte contact only with those employees of an adversary organization who have the authority to commit the organization to a position regarding the subject matter of the case?

HOLDING AND DECISION: (Cowin, J.) Yes. An attorney is banned from ex parte contact only with those employees of an adversary organization who have the authority to commit the organization to a position regarding the subject matter of the case. The employees with whom contact is prohibited are those, with "speaking authority" for the corporation who have managing authority sufficient to give them the right to speak for, and bind, the corporation. Employees who can commit the organization are those with authority to make decisions regarding the course of the litigation, such as when to initiate suit, and when to settle a pending case. The court recognizes that this test is a retrenchment from the broad prohibition on employee contact endorsed by the Massachusetts Rule of Professional Conduct which prohibits attorneys from communicating with a represented party in the absence of that party's attorney. We reject the lower court's interpretation of this rule in such manner that it would prohibit communications with any employee whose statements could be used as admissions against the organization pursuant to Fed. R. Evid. 801(d)(2)(D). Our test is consistent with the purposes of the rule, which are not to protect a corporate party from the revelation of prejudicial facts, but to protect the attorney-client relationship and prevent clients from making ill-advised statements without the counsel of their attorney. Prohibiting contact with all employees of a represented organization restricts informal contacts far more than is necessary to achieve these purposes. The test we here adopt protects an organizational party against improper advances and influence by an attorney, while still promoting access to relevant facts. While our interpretation of the rule may reduce the protection available to organizations provided by the attorney-client privilege, it allows a litigant to obtain more meaningful disclosure of the truth by conducting informal interviews with certain employees of an opposing organization. Reversed.

DISSENT: (Cordy, J.) Two of the employees of Harvard (D) had a measure of supervisory responsibility, thus their comments to the adverse attorneys were about matters within the course and scope of their employment. Accordingly, the ethics rule was violated by ex parte contact with them by opposing counsel.

ANALYSIS

As observed by the court in *Messing*, the more restrictive interpretation of the ethics rule would grant an advantage to corporate litigants over nonorganizational parties by requiring an opposing party always to seek prior judicial approval to conduct informal interviews with witnesses to an event when the opposing party happens to be an organization and the events at issue occurred at the workplace.

Quicknotes

ATTORNEY-CLIENT PRIVILEGE A doctrine precluding the admission into evidence of confidential communications between an attorney and his client made in the course of obtaining professional assistance.

EX PARTE A proceeding commenced by one party.

CHAPTER 8

Lawyer–Client Relationship

Quick Reference Rules of Law

In the Matter of Fordham

State bar (P) v. Attorney (D)

Mass. Sup. Jud. Ct., 423 Mass. 481, 668 N.E.2d 816 (1996).

NATURE OF CASE: Appeal from a ruling for defendant in case alleging excessive fees were charged by an attorney.

FACT SUMMARY: Fordham (D), an attorney representing a client charged with driving under the influence of alcohol, allegedly charged an excessively high fee.

RULE OF LAW

In determining whether fees are clearly excessive, a court may examine the difficulty of the issues presented, the time and skill required to perform the legal service properly, and the fee customarily charged in the locality for comparable services.

FACTS: The father of an accused drunk driver hired Fordham (D), an experienced litigator in a prestigious Boston law firm, to handle the case but later refused to pay the fees charged. Bar counsel charged Fordham (D) with charging a clearly excessive fee under DR 2–106(A). Fordham (D) alleged that dishonesty, bad faith or overreaching must be shown for discipline of an attorney. The hearing committee found that Fordham's (D) fee fell within a safe harbor because an agreement existed between a client and an attorney, which protected from challenge the contention that the fee was clearly excessive. Bar counsel (P) appealed to the Supreme Judicial Court.

ISSUE: In determining whether fees are clearly excessive, may a court examine the difficulty of the issues presented, the time and skill required to perform the legal service properly, and the fee customarily charged in the locality for comparable services?

HOLDING AND DECISION: (O'Connor, J.) Yes. In determining whether fees are clearly excessive, a court may examine the difficulty of the issues presented, the time and skill required to perform the legal service properly, and the fee customarily charged in the locality for comparable services. The hearing committee's and the board's determinations that a clearly excessive fee was not charged were not warranted. Neither precedent nor the disciplinary rules preclude discipline even though the amount of time Fordham (D) spent to educate himself and represent his client was spent in good faith and diligence. The mandate of DR 2–106 (B), by referring to a lawyer of ordinary prudence, creates explicitly an objective standard by which fees are to be judged. Dishonesty, bad faith or overreaching need not be established for discipline to be necessary. A public reprimand is the appropriate sanction for charging a clearly excessive fee and is appropriate in this case. Reversed.

ANALYSIS

The court in this case considered eight factors to ascertain the reasonableness of the fee. The first factor required examining the time and labor required, the novelty and difficulty of the questions involved, and the skill requisite to perform the legal service properly. Another factor considered was the fee customarily charged in the locality for similar legal services. ABA Model Rule 1.5(a) is the modern equivalent to the Model Code DR 2-106(B).

Quicknotes

PUBLIC REPRIMAND An official warning or admonition.

Committee on Professional Ethics and Conduct of Iowa State Bar Association v. Mershon

Grievance commission (P) v. Attorney (D)

Iowa Sup. Ct., 316 N.W.2d 895 (1982).

NATURE OF CASE: Review of recommendation of attorney reprimand for unethical client-business dealings.

FACT SUMMARY: Mershon (D), a lawyer, formed a corporation with a farmer client and an engineer for the development of the client's farmland as a residential township, but failed to advise his client of his adverse interests in the deal.

RULE OF LAW

Before entering into a business transaction with a client, a lawyer must obtain that client's informed consent through full disclosure.

FACTS: Mershon (D) was a lawyer who performed tax and property work for Miller, a farmer who owned 100 acres of vacant land near a Cedar Falls country club. Miller decided to develop this land as a residential township, and met with Mershon (D) and an engineer, Schenk, to discuss such a project. The men decided to form a corporation that would develop the land contingent upon their ability to borrow money based on the land as security. Miller conveyed the land to the corporation at a capitalized value of $12,500 and received 400 shares of stock. Schenk and Mershon (D) both gave the corporation their promissory notes for $12,500 and $6,250 in return for 400 and 200 shares of stock, respectively. The promissory notes were interest-free and due at the discretion of the corporation and were to represent the services provided by Schenk and Mershon (D). When the trio was unable to obtain financing unless it personally guaranteed the development loan, which they were reluctant to do, the deal fell through. Miller subsequently died, and the land was valued at $4,000/acre at his death. Mershon (D), who believed the parties had an oral understanding that if the development did not occur they would reconvey their interests in the corporation to Miller, transferred his stock to the corporation and canceled his note. Schenk, however, refused to do likewise. Despite Schenk's position, Mershon (D), as executor of Miller's will, showed Miller as sole owner of the corporate stock in the initial probate inventory. The Iowa State Bar Grievance Commission, after an investigation and hearing, decided to reprimand Mershon (D) for failing to obtain Miller's consent to his ownership in the development corporation after full disclosure. Mershon (D) appealed.

ISSUE: Before entering into a business transaction with a client, must a lawyer obtain that client's informed consent through full disclosure?

HOLDING AND DECISION: (McCormick, J.) Yes. Under DR 5–104 (A), a lawyer shall not enter into a business transaction with a client if they have differing interests therein unless the client has consented after full disclosure. Because of the fiduciary relationship between an attorney and his client, full disclosure in this context means active diligence to ensure that the client was fully informed of the nature and effect of the transaction proposed and of his own rights and interests in the subject matter involved, and by seeing to it that his client either has independent advice in the matter or else receives from the attorney such advice as the latter would have been expected to give had the transaction been one between his client and a stranger. Here, Mershon (D) and Miller plainly had differing interests. Miller's interests were aligned wholly with the development corporation. However, Mershon's (D) interests were potentially at odds with those of the corporation because his fee for legal services was tied to the value of his stock, and because he was obliged to provide such services given his debt (promissory note) to it. Although nothing was hidden from Miller by Mershon (D) and Miller was an active participant in the transaction, Mershon (D) did not advise Miller to seek independent advice, nor did he give Miller the kind of advice he would have had the transaction been conducted with a stranger. Mershon (D) did not investigate the value of his legal services to determine if it was fairly represented by his stock ownership, nor did he advise Miller to make such an estimate. There was no writing to assure that Miller would have his farm returned if the development did not proceed, or to protect him in the event of the death of Mershon (D) or Schenk. Further, the note provided by Mershon (D) contained terms highly favorable to Mershon (D). Nor did Mershon (D) advise Miller of the effect of his differing interests on the exercise of his professional judgment. Thus, although Mershon (D) did not act dishonestly or make a profit on the transaction, he did not provide Miller with full disclosure, and his reprimand was proper. Affirmed.

ANALYSIS

This case represents a judicial interpretation of what the broad and undefined requirement of "full disclosure" means under ABA Code of Professional Responsibility DR 5-104(A). However, ABA Model Rule 1.8(a), which addresses the same issue, sets forth very detailed guidelines for disclosure. Rule 1.8(a) requires the client-lawyer transaction overall to be "fair and reasonable," with "fully disclosed terms," "in writing," and with client consent "in writing" obtained after a reasonable opportunity for advice from an

Continued on next page.

outside lawyer. The Comment to Rule 1.8 also explains that the "full disclosure" rule does not apply to ordinary commercial transactions for products and services which the client routinely supplies to others. The rationale for this exception is that when the lawyer becomes one of the client's ordinary customers, the lawyer is in no position to exercise undue influence.

Quicknotes

DISCIPLINARY RULE 5-104(A) A lawyer shall not enter into a business transaction with a client if they have differing interests therein and if the client expects the lawyer to exercise his professional judgment therein for the protection of the client, unless the client has consented after full disclosure.

Jones v. Barnes

Attorney general (P) v. Convicted robber (D)

463 U.S. 745 (1983).

NATURE OF CASE: Review of grant of habeas corpus.

FACT SUMMARY: Barnes (D) contended that he had an absolute right to have his attorney on appeal raise every non-frivolous issue he requested.

RULE OF LAW

An attorney representing a defendant on appeal is not under a duty to raise every non-frivolous issue requested by the defendant.

FACTS: Barnes (D) was convicted of armed robbery. A public defender was appointed to prosecute his appeal. Barnes (D) requested that certain issues be raised in the appeal. The attorney, for reasons of strategy, declined to press all the proffered issues. The conviction was affirmed. Barnes (D) petitioned for habeas corpus, contending that his attorney's refusal to prosecute all non-frivolous issues constituted a denial of his Sixth Amendment right to counsel. The Second Circuit granted the writ, and the Supreme Court granted review.

ISSUE: Is an attorney representing a defendant on appeal under a duty to raise every non-frivolous issue requested by the defendant?

HOLDING AND DECISION: (Burger, C.J.) No. An attorney representing a defendant on appeal is not under a duty to raise every non-frivolous issue requested by the defendant. It is safe to assume that counsel is in a better position than the defendant to assess how best to prosecute an appeal. In many situations, raising every issue will be detrimental to an appeal, as the weaker points will drown the stronger ones. To create a per se rule that a defendant is entitled to have appointed counsel raise every issue he wishes would seriously undermine the ability of counsel to present the client's case in accord with counsel's professional judgment. This Court is unwilling to take such a step. Reversed.

DISSENT: (Brennan, J.) The Sixth Amendment provides that in all criminal prosecutions, the accused shall enjoy the right to have the assistance of counsel. This right seems inconsistent with a regime under which appointed counsel can refuse to raise issues with arguable merit on appeal, when the client has directed that they be raised. Clients are capable of making informed judgments about which issues to appeal, and when they do so, their choices should be respected, unless they would require lawyers to violate their consciences, the law, or their duties to the court.

ANALYSIS

It must be remembered that this was a constitutional ruling. The Court simply held that, as a matter of federal constitutional law, no right to press all issues on appeal belongs to one having appointed counsel. Depending on jurisdiction, an attorney may have an ethical obligation to raise all such issues. Canon 5 of the ABA Code of Professional Responsibility concerns an attorney's obligation to exercise independent professional judgment on behalf of such a client. This canon is primarily concerned with avoiding external, third-party influences over the attorney's decision-making process. It does not speak to interference by the client himself.

Quicknotes

HABEAS CORPUS A proceeding in which a defendant brings a writ to compel a judicial determination of whether he is lawfully being held in custody.

PER SE By itself; not requiring additional evidence for proof.

SIXTH AMENDMENT Provides the right to a speedy trial by impartial jury, the right to be informed of the accusation, to confront witnesses and to have the assistance of counsel in all criminal prosecutions.

Togstad v. Vesely, Otto, Miller & Keefe

Malpractice plaintiff (P) v. Law firm (D)

Minn. Sup. Ct., 291 N.W.2d 686 (1980).

NATURE OF CASE: Appeal of award of damages for legal malpractice.

FACT SUMMARY: Togstad (P) successfully sued Miller (D) for legal malpractice, even though she had not formally retained him.

RULE OF LAW

A retainer is not required for an attorney-client relationship that may give rise to a malpractice claim to exist.

FACTS: Mr. Togstad (P) was rendered paralyzed after a medical procedure. Fourteen months later, Mrs. Togstad (P) consulted with Miller (D) of Vesely, Otto, Miller & Keefe (D) regarding a possible medical malpractice action. After an initial consultation, Miller (D) informed Mrs. Togstad (P) that he did not think she had a case, but that he would talk to his partner. Miller (D) never called back. After Minnesota's two-year statute of limitations on medical malpractice had expired, the Togstads (P) brought a legal malpractice action against Miller (D) for giving them erroneous advice and not advising them of the two-year statute. A jury found Miller (D) to have committed malpractice and awarded over $600,000 in damages. Miller (D) and his firm (D) appealed.

ISSUE: Is a retainer required for an attorney-client relationship that may give rise to a malpractice claim to exist?

HOLDING AND DECISION: (Per curiam) No. A retainer is not required for an attorney-client relationship that may give rise to a malpractice claim to exist. The first element in a malpractice claim is the existence of an attorney-client relationship. The crux of this relationship is the provision of advice by the attorney that he either knows or should know will be followed by the person to whom he provides the advice. This does not require actual retention. Here, Mrs. Togstad (P) sought and obtained legal advice from Miller (D). It was entirely reasonable for Miller (D) to have expected the Togstads (P) to have followed his advice, which is exactly what they did. As a result, for purposes of a malpractice action, an attorney-client relationship between the Togstads (P) and Miller (D) existed. Affirmed.

ANALYSIS

It is unclear as to whether the attorney-client relationship is defined by contract or tort theory. Appellate courts around the nation have gone both ways on this issue, on a variety of grounds. The court here recognized this diversity of opinion but did not indicate its preference for one theory over the other. The court believed the contract and tort analyses for this case to be so similar that they did not need to be distinguished.

Quicknotes

RETAINER Compensation paid in advance for professional services.

CHAPTER 9

Competence

Quick Reference Rules of Law

Smith v. Lewis

Client in divorce action (P) v. Attorney (D)

Cal. Sup. Ct., 13 Cal. 3d 349, 530 P.2d 589 (1975).

NATURE OF CASE: Appeal from a jury verdict for the plaintiff in an action for legal malpractice.

FACT SUMMARY: **After Lewis (D), while representing Smith (P) in a divorce action, failed to include, as part of the community, the retirement benefits earned by Smith's (P) husband during the course of their marriage, Smith (P) brought this malpractice action against Lewis (D).**

RULE OF LAW

Even as to doubtful matters, an attorney is expected to perform sufficient research to enable him to make an informed and intelligent judgment on behalf of his client.

FACTS: Lewis (D), representing Smith (P) in a divorce action, advised Smith (P) that her husband's state and federal retirement benefits as a general in the California National Guard were not community property. Thus, the retirement benefits were not pleaded as community property and were neither considered in the litigation nor apportioned by the trial court. Lewis (D) later filed a motion to amend the decree to include the retirement benefits, but the motion was denied for untimeliness. Smith (P) consulted other counsel and, shortly thereafter, filed a malpractice action against Lewis (D). Lewis (D) contended that the law characterizing retirement benefits was so unclear at the time he represented Smith (P) that he was insulated from liability for failing to assert a claim on her behalf. The jury found for Smith (P), and Lewis (D) appealed.

ISSUE: Even as to doubtful matters, is an attorney expected to perform sufficient research to enable him to make an informed and intelligent judgment on behalf of his client?

HOLDING AND DECISION: (Mosk, J.) Yes. Even as to doubtful matters, an attorney is expected to perform sufficient research to enable him to make an informed and intelligent judgment on behalf of his client. An attorney must exercise the skill, prudence, and diligence that lawyers of ordinary skill and capacity commonly possess and exercise in the performance of the tasks which they undertake. Four years before Lewis (D) was retained by Smith (P), in *Benson v. City of Los Angeles*, 60 Cal. 2d 355 (1963), this court stated directly that "pension rights which are earned during the course of a marriage are the community property of the employee and his wife." At the time of Smith's (P) divorce action, no significant authority existed that proposed a contrary result. Lewis (D) basically rendered erroneous advice to Smith (P), contrary to her best interests, without researching readily available authority. Affirmed.

DISSENT: (Clark, J.) Even assuming that Lewis (D) negligently failed to research the pension questions, the record does not show that his negligence, rather than the uncertain status of the law and the availability of uncontested alimony, caused Smith (P) to lose a pension award.

ANALYSIS

An attorney does not ordinarily guarantee the soundness of his opinions, and accordingly, is not liable for every mistake he may make in his practice. Here the record documented Lewis's (D) failure to conduct any reasonable research into the proper characterization of retirement benefits under community property law. Instead, he assumed they were separate property not subject to community treatment and dogmatically asserted that theory, which he was unable to support with authority.

Quicknotes

ALIMONY Order for termination of payments.

COMMUNITY PROPERTY In community property jurisdictions, refers to all money or property acquired during the term of the marriage in which each spouse has an undivided one-half interest.

SEPARATE PROPERTY Property that is owned by one spouse prior to the marriage, or any income derived therefrom, and any property that is received by one spouse pursuant to a gift, devise, bequest or descent.

Strickland v. Washington

Florida attorney general (D) v. Convicted murderer (P)

466 U.S. 668 (1984).

NATURE OF CASE: Appeal from issuance of a writ of habeas corpus due to ineffective assistance of counsel.

FACT SUMMARY: **After Washington (P) was sentenced to death for his part in three brutal stabbing murders, he sought collateral relief for alleged ineffective assistance of counsel at his sentencing hearing.**

RULE OF LAW

To reverse a conviction or death sentence due to ineffective assistance of counsel, a defendant must show that counsel's performance was deficient and that such deficiency prejudiced the defense.

FACTS: After planning and committing three brutal stabbing murders, along with other crimes, Washington (P) surrendered to police, voluntarily confessing to the third murder. Against his counsel's specific advice, Washington (P) also confessed to the first two murders, waived his right to a jury trial, pleaded guilty to all charges, and waived his right to an advisory jury at his capital sentencing hearing. At that hearing, counsel did not present psychiatric evidence, choosing to emphasize Washington's (P) remorse and acceptance of responsibility. The trial judge sentenced Washington (P) to death. The Florida Supreme Court upheld the convictions. Washington (P) sought collateral relief for alleged ineffective assistance of counsel at his sentencing hearing. The district court found no prejudice from any errors in judgment made by counsel. The court of appeals reversed and remanded. The Supreme Court granted certiorari.

ISSUE: To reverse a conviction or death sentence due to ineffective assistance of counsel, must a defendant show that counsel's performance was deficient and that such deficiency prejudiced the defense?

HOLDING AND DECISION: (O'Connor, J.) Yes. To reverse a conviction or death sentence due to ineffective assistance of counsel, a defendant must show that counsel's performance was deficient and that such deficiency prejudiced the defense. The proper standard is that of reasonably effective assistance. Reasonableness must be determined on the facts of each particular case, viewed as of the time of counsel's conduct. Moreover, the reasonableness of counsel's actions may be determined or substantially influenced by the defendant's own statements or actions. Here, the conduct of Washington's (P) counsel at and before the sentencing proceeding was clearly not unreasonable. Furthermore, his strategy choice, though unsuccessful, was well within the range of professionally reasonable judgments, and the decision not to seek more character or psychological evidence than was already in hand was likewise reasonable. The judgment of the court of appeals is reversed.

DISSENT: (Marshall, J.) If counsel had further investigated the availability of mitigating evidence, he might well have decided to present some such material at the hearing. Had he done so, there is a significant chance that Washington (P) would have been given a life sentence only. Those facts are more than sufficient to establish a violation of the Sixth Amendment and to entitle Washington (P) to a new sentencing proceeding.

ANALYSIS

The purpose of the effective assistance guarantee of the Sixth Amendment is not to improve the quality of legal representation but to ensure that criminal defendants receive a fair trial. However, some commentators have argued that a higher standard than that used in *Strickland* should apply in death penalty cases. Such a standard might have required Washington's (P) attorney to actually obtain psychiatric or character evidence before discounting its usefulness.

Quicknotes

HABEAS CORPUS A proceeding in which a defendant brings a writ to compel a judicial determination of whether he is lawfully being held in custody.

MITIGATING CIRCUMSTANCES OR EVIDENCE Circumstances which may be considered as extenuating or reducing the degree of moral culpability. Although they do not constitute a justification or excuse for the offense in question they are considered in light of fairness and mercy.

SIXTH AMENDMENT Provides the right to a speedy trial by impartial jury, the right to be informed of the accusation, to confront witnesses and to have the assistance of counsel in all criminal prosecutions.

CHAPTER 10

Justice

Quick Reference Rules of Law

Unauthorized Practice of Law Committee v. Parsons Technology, Inc.

Government agency (P) v. Publisher (D)

1999 WL 47235 (N.D. Tex. 1999).

NATURE OF CASE: Rulings on motions for summary judgment.

FACT SUMMARY: Parsons Technology, Inc. (D), the publisher of Quicken Family Lawyer (QFL), was charged with violating Texas's unauthorized practice of law statute.

RULE OF LAW
The mere advising of a person as to whether or not to file a form requires legal skill and knowledge, and therefore would be the practice of law.

FACTS: The Unauthorized Practice of Law Committee (UPLC) (P) was appointed by the Texas Supreme Court to enforce Texas's unauthorized practice of law statute. The UPLC (P) alleged that the sale of a Parsons (D) computer software program entitled *Quicken Family Lawyer '99 (QFL)* violated Texas's unauthorized practice of law statute and sought to enjoin further sales. Parsons (D) removed the case to federal court and both parties moved for summary judgment. Parsons (D) alleged that the mere selling of books or software could not violate the statute because some form of personal contact beyond the contact between a publisher and a consumer is required by a plain reading of the statute. Alternatively, Parsons (D) claimed that the application of the statute to the mere sale and distribution of the software would infringe Parsons's (D) speech rights under the Texas and United States Constitutions.

ISSUE: Would the mere advising of a person as to whether or not to file a form require legal skill and knowledge, and therefore be the practice of law?

HOLDING AND DECISION: (Sanders, J.) Yes. The mere advising of a person as to whether or not to file a form requires legal skill and knowledge, and therefore would be the practice of law. Based on the interpretations of the statute by the Texas courts, *QFL* falls within the range of conduct that Texas courts have determined to be the unauthorized practice of law. No genuine issues of material fact or disputed acts exist. Parsons's (D) act of publishing *QFL* is undisputed, and the contents of *QFL* are undisputed. Furthermore, the statute passes the four-part test from *United States v. O'Brien*, 391 U.S. 367 (1968), and is constitutional. UPLC's (P) motion for summary judgment is granted.

ANALYSIS

The court in this case also held that there was no First Amendment violation. Since the purpose of the statute was to eradicate the unauthorized practice of law, its purpose had nothing to do with suppressing speech. The content-neutral statute was held not to overburden protected speech rights. A later amendment of the statute excluding computer software that clearly and conspicuously states it is not a substitute for advice from an attorney engaged in the practice of law, led to the injunction being vacated.

Quicknotes

CONTENT-NEUTRAL Refers to statutes that regulate speech regardless of its content.

FIRST AMENDMENT Prohibits Congress from enacting any law respecting an establishment of religion, prohibiting the free exercise of religion, abridging freedom of speech or the press, the right of peaceful assembly and the right to petition for a redress of grievances.

SUMMARY JUDGMENT Judgment rendered by a court in response to a motion by one of the parties, claiming that the lack of a question of material fact in respect to an issue warrants disposition of the issue without consideration by the jury.

Shapero v. Kentucky Bar Association

Attorney (P) v. State bar (D)

486 U.S. 466 (1988).

NATURE OF CASE: Review of order upholding the state bar disciplinary rule.

FACT SUMMARY: The Kentucky Bar Association (D) promulgated a disciplinary rule prohibiting the mailing of advertisements for particular legal services.

RULE OF LAW

A state may not prohibit the mailing of advertisements to a target audience believed to be in need of particular legal services.

FACTS: Shapero (P), a Kentucky attorney, applied to the Attorneys Advertising Commission of the Kentucky State Bar (D) for approval of an advertisement he wished to circulate. The advertisement would be sent to those individuals who, according to public records, were facing imminent foreclosure. The ad apprised the recipients that avenues for forestalling foreclosure existed and recommended that the addressee call Shapero's (P) office for a free consultation about their rights in this matter. While not finding the advertisement false or misleading, the Commission (D) found it to conflict with Kentucky Supreme Court Rule 3.135(5)(b)(I), which forbade direct mailing concerning a specific legal matter to one believed to require assistance as to that matter. The State Bar Ethics Committee, on appeal, agreed that the rule precluded the advertisement Shapero (P) wished to make but urged the Supreme Court of Kentucky to amend the rule. It modified the rule, but not so much as to legitimize Shapero's (P) letter. Shapero (P) brought an action seeking to have the rule declared unconstitutional. The U.S. Court of Appeals upheld the rule, and the Supreme Court granted certiorari.

ISSUE: May a state prohibit the mailing of advertisements to a target audience believed to be in need of particular legal services?

HOLDING AND DECISION: (Brennan, J.) No. A state may not prohibit the mailing of advertisements to a target audience believed to be in need of particular legal services. This Court has previously held that the First Amendment protects from state prohibition advertising that is neither false nor misleading. On the other hand, the Court has sanctioned the proscription of in-person solicitation. The factors that led this Court to conclude that solicitation could be banned were primarily the inherently coercive nature of in-person solicitation and the lack of tangible evidence, after the fact, of whether the soliciting attorney in fact overreached during the solicitation. While a direct-mail advertisement is to some extent more coercive than a general, nontargeted advertisement, the recipient in no way can be placed under the same sort of pressures that he could be in a face-to-face situation. Further, unlike in the solicitation situation, the letter itself serves as evidence of whether the advertisement is false or misleading. Since the policy reasons for prohibiting face-to-face solicitation are not present here, the speech in question is protected under the First Amendment. Reversed.

DISSENT: (O'Connor, J.) The decision today is consistent with the earlier *Zauderer v. Office of Disciplinary Counsel of Supreme Court of Ohio*, 471 U.S. 626 (1985), but that case was decided upon erroneous grounds. That case improperly applied the usual test that commercial speech is constitutionally protected if it concerns lawful activity and is neither false nor misleading. With respect to advertisements by regulated professions, the states should be free to regulate if the possibility of misleading advertisements exists. The type of advertisements at issue here, certainly contain such possibility.

ANALYSIS

A general rule of thumb can be gleaned from the Court's triumvirate of decisions, *Zauderer, Ohralik v. Ohio State Bar*, 436 U.S. 447 (1978), and the present action. It would seem that outright solicitation, face-to-face, can be categorically banned. An advertisement, even one to a target audience and containing illustrations, may be permitted. However, it must not be misleading and must disclose all or most information necessary for a would-be client to make up his mind about using the lawyer's services.

Quicknotes

COMMERCIAL SPEECH Any speech that proposes a commercial transaction, or promotes products or services.

FIRST AMENDMENT Prohibits Congress from enacting any law respecting an establishment of religion, prohibiting the free exercise of religion, abridging freedom of speech or the press, the right of peaceful assembly and the right to petition for a redress of grievances.

SOLICITATION Contact initiated by an attorney for the purpose of obtaining employment.

Gentile v. State Bar of Nevada

Attorney (D) v. State bar (P)

501 U.S. 1030 (1991).

NATURE OF CASE: Appeal from state bar disciplinary action.

FACT SUMMARY: Gentile (D) was disciplined by the State Bar of Nevada (P) for comments he made to the press about a pending criminal case in which he represented the defendant.

RULE OF LAW

Although the speech of attorneys involved in a criminal case may be more limited than that of the press at large, any such limitation must clearly give notice to those whom it is intended to affect.

FACTS: Gentile (D) represented a criminal defendant in a highly publicized trial. In an effort to counteract negative publicity, Gentile (D) held a press conference in which he claimed that his client was innocent. He stated he would prove his client's innocence by showing that the detective involved in the case committed the crime himself. He made these statements after checking into the state ethics rules and determining his remarks would not be in violation of them. Gentile's (D) client was acquitted. Nevertheless, the Nevada State Bar (P) successfully brought a disciplinary action that was upheld by the Nevada Supreme Court. The Supreme Court granted review.

ISSUE: May the speech of attorneys involved in a criminal case be more limited than that of the press at large if such limitation clearly gives notice to those whom it affects?

HOLDING AND DECISION: (Rehnquist, C.J.) Yes. The speech of attorneys involved in a criminal case may be more limited than that of the press at large if such limitations clearly give notice to those whom it affects. The First Amendment rights of those participating in a criminal trial must be balanced against the defendant's right to a fair trial. For this reason an attorney's right to comment on a case he is involved in may be "limited by the substantial likelihood of material prejudice to the impending trial."

DISSENT: (Kennedy, J.) The attempt of Model Rule 3.6 to limit speech in such a manner is void for vagueness because its safe harbor provision misled Gentile (D) into thinking he could give his press conference without fear of discipline. The rule allows general comment about the nature of the defense without elaboration but does not clearly prohibit prejudicial comment on the credibility of witnesses. As written, the rule does not give notice to those who are meant to obey the rule.

ANALYSIS

The Nevada rule was largely based on ABA Model Rule 3.6. After the *Gentile* case, the ABA amended 3.6 in order to pass constitutional scrutiny. Chief Justice Rehnquist wrote a separate opinion on the void-for-vagueness issue, which was joined by three other justices, where he found that the rule was neither vague nor overbroad.

Quicknotes

FIRST AMENDMENT Prohibits Congress from enacting any law respecting an establishment of religion, prohibiting the free exercise of religion, abridging freedom of speech or the press, the right of peaceful assembly and the right to petition for a redress of grievances.

OVERBROAD Refers to a statute that proscribes lawful as well as unlawful conduct.

CHAPTER 11

The Structure of Legal Practice

Quick Reference Rules of Law

In re Hale

Applicant (P) v. State bar (D)

Committee on Character and Fitness for the Third Appellate District of the Supreme Court of Illinois (1998).

NATURE OF CASE: Appeal from denial of the Committee on Character and Fitness to certify an applicant to the Illinois bar.

FACT SUMMARY: Hale (P), an avowed racist, successfully completed law school and passed the Illinois bar examination, but was denied certification due to an alleged lack of the requisite character and fitness for admission to the practice of law.

RULE OF LAW
To survive strict scrutiny, a significant impairment of First Amendment rights must advance a paramount interest of vital importance and the government must show the existence of such an interest.

FACTS: Hale (P), the head of a religious organization promoting white supremacy, sought admission to the practice of law in Illinois. When the committee on character and fitness (D) failed to certify him on the basis of his active advocacy of racial hatred, he appealed. Hale (P) alleged that his First Amendment rights were violated, and that he could not be excluded from a profession solely because he was a member of a particular political organization or because he held certain beliefs.

ISSUE: To survive strict scrutiny, must a significant impairment of First Amendment rights advance a paramount interest of vital importance and must the government show the existence of such an interest?

HOLDING AND DECISION: (McClintock, J.) Yes. To survive exacting scrutiny, a significant impairment of First Amendment rights must advance a paramount interest of vital importance, and the government must show the existence of such an interest. The fundamental rights guaranteed by the Constitution are paramount and of vital importance. The fundamental rights of all persons to individual dignity are so basic to the legal profession that, in the context of this case, they must be preferred over the values found in the First Amendment. A lawyer cannot, as his life's mission, do all in his power to incite racial and religious hatred among the populace so that it will peaceably abolish the rule of law for all save those of the "white race." The fundamental rights guaranteed by the Constitution have been entrusted to our courts and its officers—the lawyers. Therefore, the guardians of that trust—the judges and lawyers—cannot have as their mission in life the incitement of racial hatred in order to destroy those values. The interest advanced with respect to the role of the legal profession is paramount, and survives strict scrutiny. A balancing test may be used in public employment cases. Affirmed.

DISSENT: (Baxter, J.) Hale (P) plausibly asserts that he can hold racist views and practice law in accordance with his oath an as attorney and there is no evidence of any conduct otherwise. Until there is such conduct, the holding and even active advocacy of beliefs, no matter how repugnant to current law, cannot be the basis for denial of certification to an applicant who will subscribe to the oath.

ANALYSIS

The court in this case relied on the terms of the Declaration of Independence, the U.S. and state Constitutions, and the United Nations' Universal Declaration of Human Rights. The court noted that Hale (P) could incite racial hatred and carry out his life's mission of depriving those he dislikes of their legal right. But, the court added, he could not do so as an officer of the court.

Quicknotes

FIRST AMENDMENT Prohibits Congress from enacting any law respecting an establishment of religion, prohibiting the free exercise of religion, abridging freedom of speech or the press, the right of peaceful assembly and the right to petition for a redress of grievances.

FOURTEENTH AMENDMENT Declares that no state shall make or enforce any law which shall abridge the privileges and immunities of citizens of the United States.

FUNDAMENTAL RIGHT A liberty that is either expressly or implicitly provided for in the United States Constitution, the deprivation or burdening of which is subject to a heightened standard of review.

Grutter v. Bollinger

Law school applicant (P) v. University president (D)

539 U.S. 306 (2003).

NATURE OF CASE: Appeal from the reversal of a plaintiff's trial verdict.

FACT SUMMARY: When Barbara Grutter (P), a white Michigan resident with a 3.8 grade average and 161 LSAT score, was denied admission to the University of Michigan Law School (D), she sued the latter in federal district court, alleging racial discrimination against her in violation of the Fourteenth Amendment on the basis of the law school's (D) express consideration of race as a factor in the admissions process.

RULE OF LAW

Diversity is a compelling interest that can justify the narrowly tailored use of race in selecting applicants for admission to public universities.

FACTS: The University of Michigan Law School (D) receives more than 3,500 applications each year for a class of 350 students. To attempt to achieve student body diversity, the Law School's (D) admissions committee required admissions officials to evaluate each applicant based on all the information in the file, including a personal statement, letters of recommendation, a student's essay, GPA score, LSAT score, as well as so-called "soft variables." The admissions policy, furthermore, specifically stressed the Law School's (D) longstanding commitment to racial and ethnic diversity. In this regard, the official admission policy noted that by enrolling a "critical mass" of underrepresented minority students, the Law School (D) sought "to ensure their ability to make unique contributions to the character of the Law School." When Barbara Grutter (P), a white Michigan resident with a 3.8 grade average and 161 LSAT score, applied for admission but was denied, she sued the Law School (D) in federal district court, alleging racial discrimination against her in violation of the Fourteenth Amendment. After a 15-day bench trial, the district court upheld Grutter's (P) claim. The court of appeals reversed, and Grutter (P) appealed.

ISSUE: Is diversity a compelling interest that can justify the narrowly tailored use of race in selecting applicants for admission to public universities?

HOLDING AND DECISION: (O'Connor, J.) Yes. Diversity is a compelling interest that can justify the narrowly tailored use of race in selecting applicants for admission to public universities. Here, the Law School's (D) admissions program bears the hallmarks of a narrowly tailored plan. Truly individualized consideration demands that race be used in a flexible, nonmechanical way. It follows from this mandate that universities cannot establish quotas for members of certain racial groups or put members of those groups on separate admissions tracks. Nor can universities insulate applicants who belong to certain racial or ethnic groups from the competition for admission. Universities can, however, as was done here, consider race or ethnicity more flexibly as a "plus" factor in the context of individualized consideration of each and every applicant. The Law School's (D) goal of attaining a critical mass of underrepresented minority students does not transform its program into a quota. The evidence indicated that the Law School (D) engaged in a highly individualized, holistic review of each applicant's file, giving serious consideration to all the ways an applicant might contribute to a "diverse educational environment." Furthermore, evidence showed that the Law School (D) gives substantial weight to diversity factors besides race by frequently accepting nonminority applicants with grades and test scores lower than underrepresented minority applicants. There was no Law School (D) policy, either de facto or de jure, of automatic acceptance or rejection based on any single "soft" variable. Narrow tailoring does not require exhaustion of every conceivable race-neutral alternative. Nor does it require a university to choose between maintaining a reputation for excellence or fulfilling a commitment to provide educational opportunities to members of all racial groups. Affirmed.

CONCURRENCE: (Ginsburg, J.) From today's vantage point, one may hope, but not firmly forecast, that over the next generation's span, progress toward nondiscrimination and genuinely equal opportunity will make it safe to sunset affirmative action.

DISSENT: (Rehnquist, C.J.) The Law School's (D) means are not narrowly tailored to the interest it asserts. Stripped of its "critical mass" veil, the program is revealed as a naked effort to achieve racial balancing. As the numbers demonstrate, the Law School (D) clearly does employ racial preferences in extending offers of admission. It engages in precisely the type of racial balancing that the Court itself calls "patently unconstitutional."

DISSENT: (Kennedy, J.) The Law School (D) has not demonstrated how individual consideration is, or can be, preserved at this stage of the application process given the instruction to attain what it calls critical mass.

DISSENT: (Scalia, J.) Unlike a clear constitutional holding that racial preferences in state educational institutions are impermissible, or even a clear anticonstitutional holding, today's decision seems perversely designed to prolong the controversy and the litigation. The Constitution

Continued on next page.

proscribes government discrimination on the basis of race, and state-provided education is no exception.

DISSENT: (Thomas, J.) I believe blacks can achieve in every avenue of American life without the meddling of university administrators. The majority upholds the Law School's (D) racial discrimination not by interpreting the people's Constitution, but by responding to a faddish slogan of the cognoscenti.

ANALYSIS

As seen in *Grutter* and predecessor Supreme Court decisions, not every decision influenced by race is equally objectionable, and "strict scrutiny" is designed to provide a framework for carefully examining the importance and the sincerity of the reasons advanced by the governmental decisionmaker for the use of race in any given context.

Quicknotes

COMPELLING INTEREST TEST A standard employed by the court under strict scrutiny review to determine the constitutionality of a statute, whereby the proponent of the statute must demonstrate that classifications drawn therein serve a compelling interest and are necessary for the furtherance of a state objective.

In re Himmel

Disciplinary commission (P) v. Attorney (D)

Ill. Sup. Ct., 125 Ill. 2d 531, 533 N.E.2d 790 (1988).

NATURE OF CASE: Petition for review of recommendations made by the hearing board and review boards regarding a disciplinary complaint against a lawyer.

FACT SUMMARY: After Himmel (D) represented Forsberg in her claim against her former attorney for conversion of her personal injury settlement check, the administrator of the state disciplinary commission (P) filed a complaint against Himmel (D) for failing to report the former attorney's misconduct.

RULE OF LAW

A lawyer possessing unprivileged knowledge of a violation of the canons of ethics shall report such knowledge to a tribunal or authority empowered to investigate or act upon such violation.

FACTS: Casey, an attorney, converted the portion of a personal injury settlement check belonging to his client, Forsberg. Forsberg then retained Himmel (D) to collect her money. In return for Forsberg's agreeing not to file any criminal, civil, or attorney discipline action against him, Casey agreed to a settlement but failed to pay the amount negotiated by Himmel (D). Himmel (D) then brought suit for breach, resulting in a judgment against Casey. The administrator of the disciplinary commission (P) subsequently filed a disciplinary complaint against Himmel (D) for failing to report Casey's misconduct. The hearing board recommended a private reprimand, and the review board recommended that the complaint be dismissed. The administrator (P) sought review in the state supreme court.

ISSUE: Shall a lawyer possessing unprivileged knowledge of a violation of the canons of ethics report such knowledge to a tribunal or other authority empowered to investigate or act upon such violation?

HOLDING AND DECISION: (Stamos, J.) Yes. A lawyer possessing unprivileged knowledge of a violation of the canons of ethics shall report such knowledge to a tribunal or other authority empowered to investigate or act upon such violation. In this case, the knowledge of Casey's misconduct was not privileged since Forsberg discussed it with Himmel (D) at various times while her mother and her fiancé were present. Thus, Himmel (D) possessed unprivileged knowledge of Casey's conversion of client funds, which is illegal conduct involving moral turpitude, and failed in his duty to report such misconduct to the commission (P). Furthermore, agreeing not to prosecute or report Casey for conversion ran afoul of the criminal code's prohibition against compounding a crime. Accordingly, Himmel (D) is ordered suspended from the practice of law for one year.

ANALYSIS

This decision was widely denounced as interfering with an attorney's duty to follow a client's express instructions. Despite the mandate of DR 1-103(A) of the Model Code requiring a lawyer to report all professional misconduct, lawyers and judges generally do not report violations by other lawyers. The only two jurisdictions that do not have report requirements are California and Massachusetts.

Quicknotes

CONVERT FUNDS Depriving an owner of his funds without permission or justification.

MORAL TURPITUDE Intentional conduct demonstrating depravity or vileness and which is contrary to acceptable and traditional societal behavior.

PRIVATE REPRIMAND An official warning or admonition.

Glossary

Common Latin Words and Phrases Encountered in the Law

A FORTIORI: Because one fact exists or has been proven, therefore a second fact that is related to the first fact must also exist.

A PRIORI: From the cause to the effect. A term of logic used to denote that when one generally accepted truth is shown to be a cause, another particular effect must necessarily follow.

AB INITIO: From the beginning; a condition which has existed throughout, as in a marriage which was void ab initio.

ACTUS REUS: The wrongful act; in criminal law, such action sufficient to trigger criminal liability.

AD VALOREM: According to value; an ad valorem tax is imposed upon an item located within the taxing jurisdiction calculated by the value of such item.

AMICUS CURIAE: Friend of the court. Its most common usage takes the form of an amicus curiae brief, filed by a person who is not a party to an action but is nonetheless allowed to offer an argument supporting his legal interests.

ARGUENDO: In arguing. A statement, possibly hypothetical, made for the purpose of argument, is one made arguendo.

BILL QUIA TIMET: A bill to quiet title (establish ownership) to real property.

BONA FIDE: True, honest, or genuine. May refer to a person's legal position based on good faith or lacking notice of fraud (such as a bona fide purchaser for value) or to the authenticity of a particular document (such as a bona fide last will and testament).

CAUSA MORTIS: With approaching death in mind. A gift causa mortis is a gift given by a party who feels certain that death is imminent.

CAVEAT EMPTOR: Let the buyer beware. This maxim is reflected in the rule of law that a buyer purchases at his own risk because it is his responsibility to examine, judge, test, and otherwise inspect what he is buying.

CERTIORARI: A writ of review. Petitions for review of a case by the United States Supreme Court are most often done by means of a writ of certiorari.

CONTRA: On the other hand. Opposite. Contrary to.

CORAM NOBIS: Before us; writs of error directed to the court that originally rendered the judgment.

CORAM VOBIS: Before you; writs of error directed by an appellate court to a lower court to correct a factual error.

CORPUS DELICTI: The body of the crime; the requisite elements of a crime amounting to objective proof that a crime has been committed.

CUM TESTAMENTO ANNEXO, ADMINISTRATOR (ADMINISTRATOR C.T.A.): With will annexed; an administrator c.t.a. settles an estate pursuant to a will in which he is not appointed.

DE BONIS NON, ADMINISTRATOR (ADMINISTRATOR D.B.N.): Of goods not administered; an administrator d.b.n. settles a partially settled estate.

DE FACTO: In fact; in reality; actually. Existing in fact but not officially approved or engendered.

DE JURE: By right; lawful. Describes a condition that is legitimate "as a matter of law," in contrast to the term "de facto," which connotes something existing in fact but not legally sanctioned or authorized. For example, de facto segregation refers to segregation brought about by housing patterns, etc., whereas de jure segregation refers to segregation created by law.

DE MINIMIS: Of minimal importance; insignificant; a trifle; not worth bothering about.

DE NOVO: Anew; a second time; afresh. A trial de novo is a new trial held at the appellate level as if the case originated there and the trial at a lower level had not taken place.

DICTA: Generally used as an abbreviated form of obiter dicta, a term describing those portions of a judicial opinion incidental or not necessary to resolution of the specific question before the court. Such nonessential statements and remarks are not considered to be binding precedent.

DUCES TECUM: Refers to a particular type of writ or subpoena requesting a party or organization to produce certain documents in their possession.

EN BANC: Full bench. Where a court sits with all justices present rather than the usual quorum.

EX PARTE: For one side or one party only. An ex parte proceeding is one undertaken for the benefit of only one party, without notice to, or an appearance by, an adverse party.

EX POST FACTO: After the fact. An ex post facto law is a law that retroactively changes the consequences of a prior act.

EX REL.: Abbreviated form of the term "ex relatione," meaning upon relation or information. When the state brings an action in which it has no interest against an individual at the instigation of one who has a private interest in the matter.

FORUM NON CONVENIENS: Inconvenient forum. Although a court may have jurisdiction over the case, the action should be tried in a more conveniently located court, one to which parties and witnesses may more easily travel, for example.

GUARDIAN AD LITEM: A guardian of an infant as to litigation, appointed to represent the infant and pursue his/her rights.

HABEAS CORPUS: You have the body. The modern writ of habeas corpus is a writ directing that a person (body) being detained (such as a prisoner) be brought before the court so that the legality of his detention can be judicially ascertained.

IN CAMERA: In private, in chambers. When a hearing is held before a judge in his chambers or when all spectators are excluded from the courtroom.

IN FORMA PAUPERIS: In the manner of a pauper. A party who proceeds in forma pauperis because of his poverty is one who is allowed to bring suit without liability for costs.

INFRA: Below, under. A word referring the reader to a later part of a book. (The opposite of supra.)

IN LOCO PARENTIS: In the place of a parent.

IN PARI DELICTO: Equally wrong; a court of equity will not grant requested relief to an applicant who is in pari delicto, or as much at fault in the transactions giving rise to the controversy as is the opponent of the applicant.

IN PARI MATERIA: On like subject matter or upon the same matter. Statutes relating to the same person or things are said to be in pari materia. It is a general rule of statutory construction that such statutes should be construed together, i.e., looked at as if they together constituted one law.

IN PERSONAM: Against the person. Jurisdiction over the person of an individual.

IN RE: In the matter of. Used to designate a proceeding involving an estate or other property.

IN REM: A term that signifies an action against the res, or thing. An action in rem is basically one that is taken directly against property, as distinguished from an action in personam, i.e., against the person.

INTER ALIA: Among other things. Used to show that the whole of a statement, pleading, list, statute, etc., has not been set forth in its entirety.

INTER PARTES: Between the parties. May refer to contracts, conveyances or other transactions having legal significance.

INTER VIVOS: Between the living. An inter vivos gift is a gift made by a living grantor, as distinguished from bequests contained in a will, which pass upon the death of the testator.

IPSO FACTO: By the mere fact itself.

JUS: Law or the entire body of law.

LEX LOCI: The law of the place; the notion that the rights of parties to a legal proceeding are governed by the law of the place where those rights arose.

MALUM IN SE: Evil or wrong in and of itself; inherently wrong. This term describes an act that is wrong by its very nature, as opposed to one which would not be wrong but for the fact that there is a specific legal prohibition against it (malum prohibitum).

MALUM PROHIBITUM: Wrong because prohibited, but not inherently evil. Used to describe something that is wrong because it is expressly forbidden by law but that is not in and of itself evil, e.g., speeding.

MANDAMUS: We command. A writ directing an official to take a certain action.

MENS REA: A guilty mind; a criminal intent. A term used to signify the mental state that accompanies a crime or other prohibited act. Some crimes require only a general mens rea (general intent to do the prohibited act), but others, like assault with intent to murder, require the existence of a specific mens rea.

MODUS OPERANDI: Method of operating; generally refers to the manner or style of a criminal in committing crimes, admissible in appropriate cases as evidence of the identity of a defendant.

NEXUS: A connection to.

NISI PRIUS: A court of first impression. A nisi prius court is one where issues of fact are tried before a judge or jury.

N.O.V. (NON OBSTANTE VEREDICTO): Notwithstanding the verdict. A judgment n.o.v. is a judgment given in favor of one party despite the fact that a verdict was returned in favor of the other party, the justification being that the verdict either had no reasonable support in fact or was contrary to law.

NUNC PRO TUNC: Now for then. This phrase refers to actions that may be taken and will then have full retroactive effect.

PENDENTE LITE: Pending the suit; pending litigation under way.

PER CAPITA: By head; beneficiaries of an estate, if they take in equal shares, take per capita.

PER CURIAM: By the court; signifies an opinion ostensibly written "by the whole court" and with no identified author.

PER SE: By itself, in itself; inherently.

PER STIRPES: By representation. Used primarily in the law of wills to describe the method of distribution where a person, generally because of death, is unable to take that which is left to him by the will of another, and therefore his heirs divide such property between them rather than take under the will individually.

PRIMA FACIE: On its face, at first sight. A prima facie case is one that is sufficient on its face, meaning that the evidence supporting it is adequate to establish the case until contradicted or overcome by other evidence.

PRO TANTO: For so much; as far as it goes. Often used in eminent domain cases when a property owner receives partial payment for his land without prejudice to his right to bring suit for the full amount he claims his land to be worth.

QUANTUM MERUIT: As much as he deserves. Refers to recovery based on the doctrine of unjust enrichment in those cases in which a party has rendered valuable services or furnished materials that were accepted and enjoyed by another under circumstances that would reasonably notify the recipient that the rendering party expected to be paid. In essence, the law implies a contract to pay the reasonable value of the services or materials furnished.

QUASI: Almost like; as if; nearly. This term is essentially used to signify that one subject or thing is almost analogous to another but that material differences between them do exist. For example, a quasi-criminal proceeding is one that is not strictly criminal but shares enough of the same characteristics to require some of the same safeguards (e.g., procedural due process must be followed in a parole hearing).

QUID PRO QUO: Something for something. In contract law, the consideration, something of value, passed between the parties to render the contract binding.

RES GESTAE: Things done; in evidence law, this principle justifies the admission of a statement that would otherwise be hearsay when it is made so closely to the event in question as to be said to be a part of it, or with such spontaneity as not to have the possibility of falsehood.

RES IPSA LOQUITUR: The thing speaks for itself. This doctrine gives rise to a rebuttable presumption of negligence when the instrumentality causing the injury was within the exclusive control of the defendant, and the injury was one that does not normally occur unless a person has been negligent.

RES JUDICATA: A matter adjudged. Doctrine which provides that once a court of competent jurisdiction has rendered a final judgment or decree on the merits, that judgment or decree is conclusive upon the parties to the case and prevents them from engaging in any other litigation on the points and issues determined therein.

RESPONDEAT SUPERIOR: Let the master reply. This doctrine holds the master liable for the wrongful acts of his servant (or the principal for his agent) in those cases in which the servant (or agent) was acting within the scope of his authority at the time of the injury.

STARE DECISIS: To stand by or adhere to that which has been decided. The common law doctrine of stare decisis attempts to give security and certainty to the law by following the policy that once a principle of law as applicable to a certain set of facts has been set forth in a decision, it forms a precedent which will subsequently be followed, even though a different decision might be made were it the first time the question had arisen. Of course, stare decisis is not an inviolable principle and is departed from in instances where there is good cause (e.g., considerations of public policy led the Supreme Court to disregard prior decisions sanctioning segregation).

SUPRA: Above. A word referring a reader to an earlier part of a book.

ULTRA VIRES: Beyond the power. This phrase is most commonly used to refer to actions taken by a corporation that are beyond the power or legal authority of the corporation.

Addendum of French Derivatives

IN PAIS: Not pursuant to legal proceedings.

CHATTEL: Tangible personal property.

CY PRES: Doctrine permitting courts to apply trust funds to purposes not expressed in the trust but necessary to carry out the settlor's intent.

PER AUTRE VIE: For another's life; during another's life. In property law, an estate may be granted that will terminate upon the death of someone other than the grantee.

PROFIT A PRENDRE: A license to remove minerals or other produce from land.

VOIR DIRE: Process of questioning jurors as to their predispositions about the case or parties to a proceeding in order to identify those jurors displaying bias or prejudice.

Casenote Legal Briefs

Administrative Law .... Breyer, Stewart, Sunstein & Vermeule
Administrative Law .... Cass, Diver & Beermann
Administrative Law .... Funk, Shapiro & Weaver
Administrative Law .... Mashaw, Merrill & Shane
Administrative Law .... Strauss, Rakoff & Farina (Gellhorn & Byse)
Agency & Partnership .... Hynes & Loewenstein
Antitrust .... Pitofsky, Goldschmid & Wood
Antitrust .... Sullivan & Hovenkamp
Bankruptcy .... Warren & Bussel
Business Organizations .... Allen, Kraakman & Subramanian
Business Organizations .... Bauman, Weiss & Palmiter
Business Organizations .... Hamilton & Macey
Business Organizations .... Klein, Ramseyer & Bainbridge
Business Organizations .... O'Kelley & Thompson
Business Organizations .... Soderquist, Smiddy & Cunningham
Civil Procedure .... Field, Kaplan & Clermont
Civil Procedure .... Freer & Perdue
Civil Procedure .... Friedenthal, Miller, Sexton & Hershkoff
Civil Procedure .... Hazard, Tait, Fletcher & Bundy
Civil Procedure .... Marcus, Redish, Sherman & Pfander
Civil Procedure .... Subrin, Minow, Brodin & Main
Civil Procedure .... Yeazell
Commercial Law .... LoPucki, Warren, Keating & Mann
Commercial Law .... Warren & Walt
Commercial Law .... Whaley
Community Property .... Bird
Community Property .... Blumberg
Conflicts .... Brilmayer & Goldsmith
Conflicts .... Currie, Kay, Kramer & Roosevelt
Constitutional Law .... Brest, Levinson, Balkin & Amar
Constitutional Law .... Chemerinsky
Constitutional Law .... Choper, Fallon, Kamisar & Shiffrin (Lockhart)
Constitutional Law .... Cohen, Varat & Amar
Constitutional Law .... Farber, Eskridge & Frickey
Constitutional Law .... Rotunda
Constitutional Law .... Sullivan & Gunther
Constitutional Law .... Stone, Seidman, Sunstein, Tushnet & Karlan
Contracts .... Ayres & Speidel
Contracts .... Barnett
Contracts .... Burton
Contracts .... Calamari, Perillo & Bender
Contracts .... Crandall & Whaley
Contracts .... Dawson, Harvey, Henderson & Baird
Contracts .... Farnsworth, Young, Sanger, Cohen & Brooks
Contracts .... Fuller & Eisenberg
Contracts .... Knapp, Crystal & Prince
Copyright .... Cohen, Loren, Okediji & O'Rourke
Copyright .... Goldstein & Reese
Criminal Law .... Bonnie, Coughlin, Jeffries & Low
Criminal Law .... Boyce, Dripps & Perkins
Criminal Law .... Dressler
Criminal Law .... Johnson & Cloud
Criminal Law .... Kadish, Schulhofer & Steiker
Criminal Law .... Kaplan, Weisberg & Binder
Criminal Procedure .... Allen, Hoffmann, Livingston & Stuntz
Criminal Procedure .... Dressler & Thomas
Criminal Procedure .... Haddad, Marsh, Zagel, Meyer, Starkman & Bauer
Criminal Procedure .... Kamisar, LaFave, Israel, King & Kerr
Criminal Procedure .... Saltzburg & Capra
Debtors and Creditors .... Warren & Westbrook
Employment Discrimination .... Friedman
Employment Discrimination .... Zimmer, Sullivan & White
Employment Law .... Rothstein & Liebman
Environmental Law .... Menell & Stewart
Environmental Law .... Percival, Schroeder, Miller & Leape
Environmental Law .... Plater, Abrams, Goldfarb, Graham, Heinzerling & Wirth
Evidence .... Broun, Mosteller & Giannelli
Evidence .... Fisher
Evidence .... Mueller & Kirkpatrick
Evidence .... Sklansky
Evidence .... Waltz, Park & Friedman
Family Law .... Areen & Regan
Family Law .... Ellman, Kurtz & Scott
Family Law .... Harris, Carbone & Teitelbaum
Family Law .... Wadlington & O'Brien
Family Law .... Weisberg & Appleton
Federal Courts .... Fallon, Meltzer & Shapiro (Hart & Wechsler)
Federal Courts .... Low & Jeffries
Health Law .... Furrow, Greaney, Johnson, Jost & Schwartz
Immigration Law .... Aleinikoff, Martin & Motomura
Immigration Law .... Legomsky
Insurance Law .... Abraham
Intellectual Property .... Merges, Menell & Lemley
International Business Transactions .... Folsom, Gordon, Spanogle & Fitzgerald
International Law .... Blakesley, Firmage, Scott & Williams
International Law .... Carter, Trimble & Weiner
International Law .... Damrosch, Henkin, Murphy & Smit
International Law .... Dunoff, Ratner & Wippman
Labor Law .... Cox, Bok, Gorman & Finkin
Land Use .... Callies, Freilich & Roberts
Legislation .... Eskridge, Frickey & Garrett
Oil & Gas .... Lowe, Anderson, Smith & Pierce
Patent Law .... Adelman, Radner, Thomas & Wegner
Products Liability .... Owen, Montgomery & Davis
Professional Responsibility .... Gillers
Professional Responsibility .... Hazard, Koniak, Cramton, Cohen & Wendel
Property .... Casner, Leach, French, Korngold & VanderVelde
Property .... Cribbet, Johnson, Findley & Smith
Property .... Donahue, Kauper & Martin
Property .... Dukeminier, Krier, Alexander & Schill
Property .... Haar & Liebman
Property .... Kurtz & Hovenkamp
Property .... Nelson, Stoebuck & Whitman
Property .... Rabin, Kwall & Kwall
Property .... Singer
Real Estate .... Korngold & Goldstein
Real Estate Transactions .... Nelson & Whitman
Remedies .... Laycock
Remedies .... Shoben, Tabb & Janutis
Securities Regulation .... Coffee, Seligman & Sale
Securities Regulation .... Cox, Hillman & Langevoort
Sports Law .... Weiler & Roberts
Taxation (Corporate) .... Lind, Schwartz, Lathrope & Rosenberg
Taxation (Individual) .... Burke & Friel
Taxation (Individual) .... Freeland, Lathrope, Lind & Stephens
Taxation (Individual) .... Klein, Bankman, Shaviro & Stak
Torts .... Dobbs, Hayden & Bublick
Torts .... Epstein
Torts .... Franklin & Rabin
Torts .... Henderson, Pearson, Kysar & Siliciano
Torts .... Schwartz, Kelly & Partlett (Prosser)
Trademark .... Ginsburg, Litman & Kevlin
Wills, Trusts & Estates .... Dukeminier, Sitkoff & Lindgren
Wills, Trusts & Estates .... Dobris, Sterk & Leslie
Wills, Trusts & Estates .... Scoles, Halbach, Roberts & Begleiter

CPSIA information can be obtained at www.ICGtesting.com
Printed in the USA
LVOW09s0233080915

453222LV00019B/334/P